THE LONDON THEOLOGICAL LIBRARY

UNDER THE EDITORSHIP OF

PROFESSOR ERIC S. WATERHOUSE, D.Lit., D.D.

AN INTRODUCTION TO
THE NEW TESTAMENT

THE LONDON THEOLOGICAL LIBRARY

Under the Editorship of
PROFESSOR ERIC S. WATERHOUSE,
D.Lit., D.D.

AN INTRODUCTION TO
THE NEW TESTAMENT

By

FRANK BERTRAM CLOGG
M.A., B.D. (Cantab.), B.D. (Lond.)
Sometime Scholar of Emmanuel College, Cambridge
Professor in New Testament Language and Literature
in the University of London

LONDON:

UNIVERSITY OF LONDON PRESS, Ltd.
HODDER AND STOUGHTON, Ltd.

FIRST PRINTED	.	.	.	.	1937
SECOND EDITION	.	.	.	.	1940
Reprinted	.	.	.	1943,	1945
THIRD EDITION	.	.	.	.	1948
Reprinted	.	.	.	.	1949

Printed & Bound in England for the UNIVERSITY OF LONDON PRESS, LTD.,
by HAZELL, WATSON & VINEY, LTD., Aylesbury and London

PREFACE TO THE THIRD EDITION

THREE Appendices have been printed in this edition. Appendix I has additional notes on Ch. I—the date of Polycarp's Epistles : and on Ch. IV, XVIII, XIX from some recent lectures by T. W. Manson on Galatians, Mark and Matthew.

Appendix II gives a translation of the oldest anti-Marcionite Prologues to the Gospels : Appendix III gives a translation of other early witnesses to the Books of the New Testament, to which reference is made in this book.

One or two minor changes have also been made in this edition, and the names of some recent books have been inserted in the Bibliography.

F. B. C.

RICHMOND COLLEGE,
March 1948

PREFACE TO THE SECOND EDITION

THE printing of a second edition has given the opportunity of making a number of corrections. A few alterations and additions on important points will be found on pages 9, 54, 65, 80, 179, 196, 214–215, 242, 265–266, and in the Bibliography, pages 298–300.

F. B. C.

RICHMOND COLLEGE,
February 1940

PREFACE

To try in a small volume to estimate the value of the work of many scholars in the wide field of New Testament criticism is no light task. This book is the result of a reverent and diligent, though far from complete, study of the literature which has grown up around the New Testament. It sets out to show how the several books came to their present form, and to examine the literary and historical problems which the study of them raises. And since the purpose of all such study is to throw light upon the meaning of the books, it offers, not so much an analysis of what each contains, but a brief exposition of its permanent value and of its message for us to-day.

Of necessity there are many interesting theories which may seem dismissed in a sentence or passed over in silence ; and I am conscious of my debt to many scholars whose names have not even been mentioned in the pages that follow. But a short Bibliography has been added to call attention to some of the more important books, especially to those more recently published in English. Many of these are to be commended, not only to the student, but to the general reader.

My thanks are due especially to my friends the Rev. Dr. W. F. Howard and the Rev. Dr. H. G. Meecham. The former read part of the typescript and made many valuable suggestions. The latter read the proofs verified the references, and by his kindly criticism helped much towards clearness of thought and of expression

Last, but not least, I gratefully acknowledge the help
which my wife, my daughter, and my son have given me
in reading the proofs and in the checking of the references in the index.

F. B. C.

RICHMOND COLLEGE,
    August 1936

CONTENTS

PART III

THE EPISTLE TO THE HEBREWS

PART IV

THE CATHOLIC EPISTLES

PART V

THE SYNOPTIC GOSPELS AND ACTS

PART VI

THE JOHANNINE WRITINGS

PART I

THE TRANSMISSION OF THE TEXT AND THE GROWTH OF THE CANON

CHAPTER I

THE TRANSMISSION OF THE TEXT AND THE GROWTH OF THE CANON

The twenty-seven books which make up the New Testament were written in Greek in the latter half of the first or in the early years of the second century A.D. Many of these books are in the form of letters sent to small societies in various cities of the Roman Empire, letters full of practical exhortation, which however their writers hardly intended to be regarded as theological treatises or books of devotion.[1] The other books of the New Testament, the four Gospels and Acts, have no exact analogies in contemporary literature. They were written with an aim, partly historical, partly apologetic, to explain how men came to believe in Jesus as the Christ, and in order that men might believe, written for local Christian Churches, when the generation of those who had been " eye-witnesses and ministers of the word " was passing, or had already passed.

[1] " The most striking marvel in the scattered writings of the New Testament is the perfect fitness which they exhibit for fulfilling an office of which their authors appear themselves to have had no conception."— Westcott, *Introduction to the Study of the Gospels*, p. 166.

The autographs, none of which has been preserved, would have been written on papyrus rolls,
which in the case of the longer books would have
been about thirty feet in length.   Copies were made
of them on papyrus, until the fourth century, when
vellum codices took the place of papyrus rolls.
From recent discoveries it is known that copies were
made as early as the second century on papyrus
codices, but the roll form was more often used
in the papyrus age.   No doubt the change from
the roll to the codex, i.e. book form, and especially
the change to the more convenient and durable
vellum codex, facilitated the collection of the books
of the New Testament into one volume, and had
some influence on the growth of the Canon.

The letters of the New Testament were dictated.
In that, and in the form and style, they are akin
to the many fragments of contemporary papyrus
letters which have been discovered and studied in
the last half-century.   Most probably the other
books of the New Testament were similarly dictated
to experienced, if not to professional, scribes in the
first instance.   The letters would have been carried
to their destination by trusted friends—hence the
importance of Titus in the correspondence of Paul.
There was an imperial but not a general post.   The
multiplication of copies of the original writings was

due to practical needs. The process of copying inevitably led to corruptions in the text, especially in the earliest years, before the writings were regarded as having canonical authority, and when the importance of preserving each word and letter was not yet recognized. Dating from the fourth century onwards there is a large number of Greek manuscripts, more than 4,000 in all, of the whole or parts of the New Testament, all copied by hand, until in 1516 Froben of Basel issued the first printed Greek Testament, having commissioned Erasmus to prepare the text.[1] Since that time many editions of the Greek text have been printed by different editors, of which the edition of Westcott and Hort in 1881 is the most important, because they for the first time worked out systematically the general principles on which the reconstruction of the original text must be based.

The Text and its Transmission. Our knowledge of the text is derived from three sources : (1) Greek Manuscripts ; (2) The Versions ; (3) The Fathers.

(1) The vellum Greek manuscripts are divided into (*a*) Uncials, which date from the fourth century onwards ; (*b*) Minuscules, which are not older than

---

[1] The N.T. volume of the Complutensian Polyglot was printed in 1514, but was not published until 1522.

the ninth century. These names are derived from the different styles of writing, the one superseding the other. Within the last few years about fifty manuscripts of the Greek Testament, mostly fragmentary, written on papyrus, have been discovered. The oldest of these date from the second century.[1]

(2) The most important of the Versions, i.e. the translations of the Greek text into other languages, are :

(a) The Latin Versions : (i) The Old Latin, which was a translation made as early as the second century ; (ii) The Vulgate, a revision of the Old Latin made by Jerome at the end of the fourth century. The Vulgate exists to-day in about 8,000 manuscripts, and is the standard text for the Roman Church.

(b) The Syriac Versions. The two most important of the four which exist are : (i) The Old Syriac, which is as old as the second century, but of which little except the Gospels has survived ; (ii) The Peshitto, a revision of the Old Syriac made probably in the fifth century.

(c) The Egyptian, or Coptic Versions, of which the most important are the Bohairic and the Sahidic.

[1] C. H. Roberts assigns a date between A.D. 130 and 150 to *An Unpublished Fragment of the Fourth Gospel in the John Rylands Library.*

Neither of these is probably older than the third century.

The other ancient Versions, such as the Armenian, Ethiopic, and Gothic, are later and of less value to the textual critic.

(3) The evidence of the Fathers is to be found in their commentaries on the books of the New Testament and in their writings generally.

The importance of the evidence of the Versions and of the Fathers is that they sometimes bear witness to a text that is earlier than our earliest Greek manuscripts; that we can learn from them what type of text was current in different churches, and at what date.

Westcott and Hort classified these authorities into groups or families of texts, four in number, to which they gave the following names : (1) Western—the name is not geographical—a type of text everywhere prevalent in the second century, of which the most famous representative for the Gospels and Acts is Codex Bezae (fifth or sixth century); (2) Alexandrian, a local text current in Alexandria, whose variations are not very important; (3) Neutral, which, as the name implies, is free from primitive corruptions. The best representatives of this are Codex Vaticanus and Codex Sinaiticus (fourth century); (4) Syrian. To this the great mass of manuscripts belongs. But since it does not appear until the Fathers of the fourth century, and seems to be a revision based upon the Western and the Neutral, it can for the most part be set aside as of secondary value.

Since Westcott and Hort's time the discovery of the Sinaitic Syriac—another authority for the Old Syriac Version of the Gospels, and for the Western text ; of the Freer Manuscript of the Gospels, now in Washington ; of the Koridethi Codex ; and more recently of the Chester Beatty Papyri, which contain considerable portions of the Gospels, Acts, Pauline Epistles, and Apocalypse—has given additional material of great value for the study of the text. The result of this has been (1) to confirm Hort's judgment of the relative unimportance of the Syrian, or, as it is now called, the Byzantine type of text ; (2) to make it probable that the Alexandrian, as Hort called it, is not a separate family, but that the Neutral text represented by the Vaticanus and the Sinaiticus was the local text of Alexandria. The name now given to this family is Alexandrian, instead of Neutral. It is not as pure in transmission as Westcott and Hort thought, but has probably been treated by an editor who conscientiously tried to establish the original text ; (3) to show that the so-called Western is not a single text, but a group of local texts, one representing Italy and Africa, another Caesarea, and another the Syriac-speaking Church.[1]

In conclusion, the Alexandrian is still regarded as the best of the local texts, especially for the Gospels, and any attempt to reconstruct the original will be based on the Vaticanus and the Sinaiticus; but it is allowed that more attention must be paid to the Western text, especially to the Caesarean form of it, than Westcott and Hort, with the evidence before them, were prepared to admit.

The most important critical editions of the Greek Testament since Westcott and Hort have been: (1) Novum Testamentum Graece—Alexander Souter, 1910—the Greek text behind the Revised Version with critical apparatus[2]; (2) the edition of H. von Soden, 1902–1913, a work of much erudition which proved a disappointment because the editor attached too much importance to the *Diatessaron* of Tatian, which is known to us in very imperfect copies, and because he paid too little attention to evidence of the Versions and the Fathers; (3) the edition of Eberhard Nestle, printed in 1898, based upon the editions of Westcott and Hort, Tischendorf, and Weymouth. In the later editions Bernard Weiss's edition was sub-

[1] *v.* F. G. Kenyon, *The Text of the Greek Bible*, pp. 210–240.
[2] Editio altera 1947.

stituted for that of Weymouth. Erwin Nestle revised his father's work, and issued a new edition in 1930, based upon the same three earlier texts together with that of von Soden.[1]

The Growth of the Canon. The Christian Church inherited a body of sacred Scriptures, the Old Testament, from the Jews, and while in course of time the existence of the Old Testament facilitated the recognition of a new body of Scripture, it must at first have retarded it. The Old Testament was equally accessible to the Gentile as to the Jewish Christians in the Greek Version, the Septuagint, and supplied at first all the needs of the Church, the facts of our Lord's life being made known by oral teaching. Perhaps the earliest Christian book was a collection of Old Testament passages to prove that Jesus was the Messiah, and some such book may have been used by more than one writer in the New Testament.[2] But from the beginning the words of Jesus took their place beside the Old Testament and were held in equal authority with it.[3] It was not long before the books which recorded His

[1] A new critical edition of the Greek Testament is being published by the Oxford Press. The Gospel of Mark appeared in 1935, edited by S. C. E. Legg. The Gospel of Matthew appeared in 1940.

[2] *v.* Rendel Harris, *Testimonies*, pt. i, pt. ii.

[3] *v.* Acts xx. 35 ; 1 Cor. vii. 10, 12, ix. 14 ; 1 Tim. v. 18. *v.* Jülicher-Fascher, *Einleitung in das Neue Testament*, s. 457.

words were read in the Services of the Church alongside the Old Testament.[1]   But before the Gospels were even written, the letters of Paul were read as they were received in the churches to which they were sent.   When Paul was dead, and the letters he had written were collected, they were doubtless read in the public Services of the Church, and so were put side by side with the Law and the Prophets. The Apostles were the witnesses and interpreters of Christian doctrine, and their writings came to be regarded, with the Gospels, as the standard for the teaching of Christian truth and the regulation of Christian practice and discipline.   Probably the first to define a Canon of Christian writings was the Gnostic, Marcion, who accepted an Evangelion, the Gospel of Luke, omitting passages which did not agree with his views, and an Apostolicon, ten Epistles of Paul.

The history of the Canon falls into three periods. The first is from the time when the books were written until the end of the second century. It includes the era of separate circulation and the gradual collection of the Apostolic writings.   The evidence for the existence of the several books and of the authority attached to them (which is not the same thing) in this period is found : in the Epistle

[1] Justin, *Apol.*, i. 65.

of Clement of Rome to the Corinthians, *c.* A.D. 96 ; the Epistles of Ignatius and Polycarp, *c.* 115 ; the Didache, the date of which is disputed : it is not safe to put it earlier for this purpose than *c.* 130 ; the Epistle of Barnabas and the Shepherd of Hermas, which were probably written in the early years of the second century ; Papias, whose work is known to us through Eusebius, *c.* 140–150 ; Justin Martyr, who wrote in Rome between *c.* 153 and 165 ; Tatian, whose Diatessaron was published *c.* 175 ; Marcion, whose Canon may be dated *c.* 140–150.

The conclusion of this period is marked by the acknowledgment throughout the Christian Church of a large part of our New Testament as authoritative Scripture—the Four Gospels, Acts, Thirteen Epistles of Paul (excluding Hebrews), and 1 John and 1 Peter, although these last were not everywhere acknowledged. Seven books still lacked general recognition, Hebrews, James, 2 Peter, 2 and 3 John, Jude, and the Apocalypse ; while other books, such as the Epistle of Barnabas, the Shepherd of Hermas, and the Didache, were also on the fringe of the Canon. The evidence for the end of the second century is derived from Irenaeus, representing the Church in Gaul, 181–189 ; Clement of Alexandria, 190–210 ; Tertullian, representing the Church in North Africa, 195–220 ; the Muratorian Fragment, which gives what was probably the Canon of the Church of Rome. It is a Latin translation of the Greek original which may have been written by Hippolytus, and the date is *c.* 200.

The second period of the Canon is from *c.* 200 to 325, when, largely through the influence of Origen and Eusebius, there was a sifting of the books on the fringe, some of which came to be included and others ultimately rejected.

The third period of the Canon begins in 325, and is marked by authoritative pronouncements, first by individuals, no doubt representing local churches, and later by Councils. In the East Athanasius was the first to put forward a Canon, exactly coinciding with our New Testament, in his Paschal Letter A.D. 367; in the West the Council of Carthage in 397. By the end of the fourth century the New Testament was practically fixed in the form in which we have it now, but for another century there were doubts still existing about the shorter Catholic Epistles and the Apocalypse in Asia Minor and the Syriac-speaking Churches. The Quini-Sextine Council[1] confirmed the present Canon for East and West, but no Oecumenical Council has ever pronounced upon it. From our knowledge of the Christian literature of the early Church it is agreed

---

[1] At Constantinople in A.D. 692.

that the Spirit of Truth did guide the Church in selecting all that was most worth preserving. " The authority " (of the writers of these books) " on the things of God, which the test of centuries has only enhanced, ranks higher for us than that of any other writers in the world. The New Testament is a collection of masterpieces of spiritual music. Its authority is that of spiritual experts, and we treat it as we should treat the authority of any supreme expert *on his subject*." [1]

[1] A. H. McNeile, *Introduction to the New Testament*, p 471.

PART II
THE PAULINE EPISTLES

CHAPTER II

THE EPISTLES TO THE THESSALONIANS

According to Acts xvii. 1 Paul and his companions, Silas and Timothy, came to Thessalonica after their release from imprisonment at Philippi. Thessalonica was on the main road, the Via Egnatia, and had a synagogue, two things which may have drawn Paul to stay there. It seems to have been his practice to stay for a time at cities separated from each other some distance, but on the main trade routes, making them centres from which the Gospel might reach the surrounding district. According to Acts Paul reasoned in the synagogue for three sabbath days proving that the Messiah was destined to suffer and that the Messiah was Jesus.[1] He made a number of converts among the Jews and among the Gentile proselytes, and particularly among the leading women of the town.[2] It is known that in Macedonia women had a better social position than anywhere else in the civilized world. And as a small mark of the accuracy of the author of Acts we find women at Philippi, Thessalonica, and Beroea prominent in connexion with the activity of the Apostles.

[1] xvii. 2, 3.   [2] xvii. 4.

The Jews, jealous of his success, roused the rabble to attack the house where Paul and Silas lodged. They had been warned in time, but Jason, their host, was brought before the politarchs. The accuracy of Acts is shown again in this local word for the Thessalonian magistrates, which has been verified by inscriptions. Probably Paul had emphasized in his preaching the Coming of the Lord to judge the world, and this gave his enemies the chance of making the dangerous accusation " these who have upset the world have come here too, who act contrary to the decrees of the Emperor, saying there is another king, Jesus." This was the first time that accusation had been made since Pilate signed the death-warrant of our Lord.

The politarchs bound over Jason to keep the peace, and made him deposit a sum of money as guarantee. Paul and Silas would have brought Jason into serious trouble, unless they had left the city. They meant to return probably as soon as new magistrates came into office. But in this they were disappointed, for we read in 1 Thess. ii. 18, "We would fain have come unto you, I Paul once and again; and Satan hindered us." Leaving Thessalonica, Paul and his fellow-missionaries went to Beroea ; their success there was cut short by the arrival of Jews from Thessalonica who caused them trouble. Paul was taken to Athens, the others were left behind. After preaching in Athens Paul went on to Corinth, where he stayed a year and a half.[1] It appears from 1 Thess. iii. 2 that Timothy rejoined Paul in Athens, and was sent back from there to Thessalonica. Before he returned Paul had gone to Corinth, where Timothy and Silas found him, and brought him news of the Thessalonian converts. This news led him to write these two letters, or at any rate the first of them.

THE FIRST EPISTLE TO THE THESSALONIANS. *Authenticity.*—The evidence for the Pauline authorship of this letter is convincingly strong. The existence of 2 Thessalonians certainly implies Paul's authorship of 1 Thessalonians. It was included by Marcion in his Canon; it is mentioned in the Muratorian Fragment. Irenaeus is the first to quote it by name, and there appears to have been no doubt about its genuineness until the time of F. C. Baur and the Tübingen school. The only authentic Epistles according to Baur were those which dealt with the Judaistic controversy. Judged by that standard, these two letters are not genuine, but no one does judge by that standard to-day.

Surely no later writer would have attributed to

---

[1] Acts xviii. 11.

Paul the belief that the Parousia would happen in his lifetime. The problem of those who died between their conversion and the Parousia could have been acute only at a very early stage ; clearly some answer must have been given to it before whole generations of Christians had died, and still the Lord had not come. The organization of the Church is in a very rudimentary stage, and there is no motive apparent which can explain the invention of the letter by a later writer.

It must, however, be admitted that in important particulars the letter does not quite agree with the narrative of Acts.

(1) In Acts xvii. 2 " three sabbaths " are mentioned, but in 1 Thess. ii. 7–11 it appears Paul had worked at his trade while in Thessalonica, and the impression is that he had lived there for some months at least. This is supported by Phil. iv. 16, where he mentions that he had twice received gifts from Philippi while he was in Thessalonica.

(2) In Acts xvii. 4, the converts are Jews and Gentiles ; in 1 Thess. i. 9, ii. 14, iv. 1–5 he makes it clear that the readers are Gentiles: " Ye turned unto God from idols."

(3) In Acts xviii. 5 Silas and Timothy rejoin Paul at Corinth ; in 1 Thess. iii. 1 ff. Timothy was with him at Athens and was sent from there back to

Thessalonica, rejoining Paul again after he reached Corinth.

Discrepancies of this nature prove little except that the authors of Acts and of 1 Thessalonians wrote independently of each other.

The Purpose and Value of the Epistle. Paul was already a missionary of many years' experience when he wrote this letter. He had been disquieted by the news that he received from Thessalonica. He is careful to stress three points about the message and the messengers. First, the message was the word of God,[1] the revelation of His purpose in Christ, Who died and rose again. Secondly, Paul recalls the character of the preachers who were the means by which the divine message reached his readers.[2] Here he is evidently meeting charges which had been made against the missionaries. " Ye know what manner of men we shewed ourselves toward you for your sake. And ye became imitators of us, and of the Lord." [3] The message would have suffered if the messengers could be justly accused of impure motives, of self-seeking, of error, guile, or flattery. On the contrary, they had been gentle, affectionate, " well pleased to impart unto you, not the gospel of God only, but also our own souls." [4] Thirdly, the message was given that

---

[1] 1 Thess. ii. 13 ff.   [2] ii. 1–12.   [3] i. 5, 6.   [4] ii. 8.

those who heard might be delivered from the doom that awaits a godless life, and enter into fellowship with God in a way of life which was according to the pattern of the Incarnate Life.

The letter was written to encourage the Thessalonians to persevere in love towards one another and to all men ; to admonish the disorderly, especially those who had allowed the Advent hope to be an excuse for slackness, for playing truant.[1]   About this Advent hope they needed further instruction. They were troubled because some of their loved ones were dying, and still the Lord had not come. Paul writes : " The Lord Himself shall descend from heaven, with a shout, with the voice of the archangel, and with the trump of God : and the dead in Christ shall rise first ; then we that are alive, that are left, shall together with them be caught up in the clouds to meet the Lord in the air ; and so shall we ever be with the Lord." [2]

This apocalyptic hope belongs to a world of thought very different from ours. But it taught men to believe that it was not only the past in which Jesus had shown His lordship, but the future was His also ; that the Kingdom of God would be established on the earth by the manifestation of supernatural

---

[1] v. 14, νουθετεῖτε τοὺς ἀτάκτους.   [2] iv. 16, 17.

powers.   As Paul expresses it, this hope has high ethical value.   "The day of the Lord so cometh as a thief in the night" [1]—"let us not sleep, let us watch and be sober." [2]   "May your spirit and soul and body be preserved entire, without blame at the coming of our Lord Jesus Christ.   Faithful is he that calleth you, who will also do it." [3]   Paul is here the pastor rather than the theologian, and his message may be summed up, "Whether we wake or sleep, we live together with Christ"—that is the one thing that matters.

THE SECOND EPISTLE TO THE THESSALONIANS. *Authenticity.*—The external evidence for this is equally as good as for the first epistle.   Polycarp, Ignatius, and Justin seem to have known it. Marcion and the Muratorian Fragment include it with Paul's Epistles ; Irenaeus quotes it by name. After that date it is universally accepted.

But its genuineness has been questioned by others than the Tübingen school.   It is said that its eschatology is inconsistent with that of 1 Thessalonians ; that, whereas the first letter makes no use of the Old Testament, this is entirely Jewish in colouring ; and that its tone is colder and more formal.   There is, besides, the difficulty of knowing why Paul should have written two letters in terms so

---

[1] v. 2.   [2] v. 6.   [3] v. 23.

similar and after so short an interval to the same Church.

Those who deny on these grounds the authenticity of this letter find it difficult to suggest why anyone should have written a pseudonymous letter, in the name of Paul, shortly after his death, (the date must be earlier than A.D. 70), about an eschatological point which would not have been a serious question at that time.

The Jewish tone led Harnack to offer an ingenious defence of its genuineness. He suggested that this letter was written to the Jewish section of the Church, while the first letter was written to the Gentile section. His argument is based on a variant reading in 2 Thess. ii. 13 : " God chose you as a first-fruit." [1] The Thessalonians were not the first Christians in Macedonia ; but the Jews were the first converts in Thessalonica ; and the Christian Jews could be called the first-fruit of the Gospel in the city. Harnack thinks there are traces of a division in the community by the stress on the word " all " in 1 Thess. v. 26–27. He further suggests that after the address " to the Church of the Thessalonians " the phrase " who are of the circumcision " [2] has fallen out. This theory meets some of the objections, but we have no evidence elsewhere

---

[1] ἀπ' ἀρχῆς. v.l. ἀπαρχήν.   [2] τῶν ἐκ τῆς περιτομῆς i. 1.

that a Church was ever divided into two communities.

But without Harnack's defence there are no insuperable difficulties in accepting the genuineness of this letter. Such difficulties as there are come from our ignorance of the situation. The letter seems to have been written because the Thessalonians were either misunderstanding his first letter, or had received a letter supposed to have come from Paul, stating that the Day of the Lord had come (2 Thess. ii. 2). It is in reference to this that the "little apocalypse," 2 Thess. ii. 3–12, is written. In the first letter he had seemed to imply that the Parousia was imminent; in this letter he says that first will come a great "apostasy," and the revelation of the "man of lawlessness."[1] The difference is one of emphasis. In 1 Thessalonians he says the Day is very near and will come suddenly. In this letter he implies that certain great events will happen first. It is reasonable to suppose that the Apostle is correcting a misapprehension, or possibly a wilful misrepresentation, of the eschatology of the first letter, rather than that he is correcting the eschatology itself.

The Little Apocalypse. This little apocalypse[2] is clearly the most important passage in the letter.

---

[1] ὁ ἄνθρωπος τῆς ἀνομίας. v.l. τῆς ἁμαρτίας.   [2] ii. 3–12.

The meaning seems to be that before the Advent of the Lord the power of evil will be unchained : at present it is under restraint ; and then the Lord Jesus will slay the evil one with the breath of His mouth. To understand this it must be remembered that the Jews, Paul with them, believed that as there had been war in heaven before the creation, so there would be at the end of the age. Some defier of God would arise, the antithesis of the Messiah. The Apostle calls him the " man of lawlessness " or " man of sin." ἀνομία (lawlessness) is used in the LXX in 2 Sam. xxii. 5 to translate Belial or Beliar, an angel of the abyss in Babylonian mythology. What the apostle seems to mean is a current idea of Anti-Christ which had been coloured by this myth. Possibly his conception of the blasphemy, which this " man of Beliar " would act, may have been coloured by Caligula's attempt to set up his statue in the Temple [1]—" he sitteth in the temple of God, setting himself forth as God." But while the mystery of lawlessness is already at work there is " one that restraineth " who is also indicated in the neuter gender.[2] The most likely meaning of this is the Roman power which could be described as " that which restraineth," or " he that restraineth," the Roman Emperor, in whom that power was

[1] A.D. 41.   [2] ὁ κατέχων (7) : τὸ κατέχον (6).

concentrated.   When that power is removed, then Anti-Christ will be revealed and slain by Christ. It is clear that the conception of Anti-Christ here owes nothing to the Nero Redivivus legend, which is found in connexion with it in the Apocalypse. So that most of those who doubt the Pauline authorship of this letter agree that it was written before A.D. 70.

The language of apocalyptic was studiedly vague and cautious—it was wiser to use symbols than real names—and we may not be certain about the interpretation.   But it bears witness to the reality of the struggle between good and evil, and to the hope in the final triumph of good.   It sanctions belief that the struggle between good and evil works itself out in contemporary events and becomes palpable and incarnate, and that the Kingdom of God will be established, not by the slow result of evolution, but by the emergence of supernatural forces.

CHAPTER III

THE FIRST AND SECOND EPISTLES TO THE CORINTHIANS

Paul's Relations with Corinth by Letter and by Visit.
1. Paul came from Athens to Corinth, the *Vanity Fair* of Greece, on his second journey and lived with Aquila and Priscilla, working with them at his trade (Acts xviii. 1 ff.). "He reasoned in the synagogue every sabbath, and persuaded Jews and Greeks." When Timothy and Silas rejoined him he was constrained by the word, testifying to the Jews that the Messiah is Jesus. This produced such opposition that he declared he would go to the Gentiles. He left the house of Aquila and lodged with a Gentile proselyte, Titus Justus, whose house was near the synagogue.[1] Crispus, the ruler of the synagogue, believed, and many of the Corinthians. "But when Gallio was proconsul," says Acts, seeming to imply that Gallio entered upon his office after the arrival of the Apostle. An inscription fixes the date of Gallio's arrival as July, A.D. 52.[2] Probably it was soon after his

[1] Perhaps Acts xviii. 7 means that Paul conducted a rival service in the house of Titus Justus. *v.* Foakes Jackson and Kirsopp Lake, *The Beginnings of Christianity*, vol. iv. 225.

[2] There is some doubt about this. Deissmann gives July, A.D. 51; Lake, in *The Beginnings of Christianity*, vol. v. 464, is undecided between 51 and 52; Bultmann gives 52–53.

coming, and it may be because of his gentle character, which the Jews mistook for weakness, that the Jews seized the occasion for bringing a charge against Paul. " This man persuadeth men to worship God contrary to the law." [1] As soon as Gallio discovered that the charge was religious, not political, he dismissed it with contempt. The mob did not lose their opportunity of Jew-baiting, but the Apostle was not their victim ; the proconsul " cared for none of these things." Shortly after the Apostle crossed by sea to Ephesus together with Aquila and Priscilla, whom he left there. He himself went on to Caesarea, and perhaps to Jerusalem, and then to Antioch.[2] After some time there he started again on his third missionary journey, and came to Ephesus.[3]

2. After Paul had left Ephesus the former time, an Alexandrian Jew, Apollos, came there, and was instructed in the truth of Christianity by Priscilla and Aquila. He was minded to go to Corinth, and was commended to the Corinthian Church by Priscilla and Aquila. It may be presumed that he was continuing Paul's work there, when the latter returned to Ephesus.

3. Something untoward seems to have occurred to cause Apollos to leave Corinth and to return to

[1] xviii. 13.   [2] xviii. 22.   [3] xix. 1.

Ephesus. Whatever it was, it was of such a character that he was reluctant to visit Corinth again, when 1 Cor. xvi. 12 was written. Perhaps other teachers had arrived at Corinth hostile to Paul and Apollos.

4. Because of disquieting news brought, perhaps by Apollos, from Corinth, Paul wrote a letter warning the Corinthians against associating with immoral persons (1 Cor. v. 9). (*The Previous Letter*, possibly 2 Cor. vi. 14–vii. 1 is a fragment of this letter.)

5. The Apostle learned of the state of the Corinthian Church from members of the household of Chloe, presumably a rich lady who had connexions with both Ephesus and Corinth; and from three Corinthians, Fortunatus, Achaicus, and Stephanas, who had come to Ephesus with a letter for the Apostle asking questions of doctrinal and practical importance. What he learned caused the Apostle to write 1 Corinthians, dealing in chs. i–vi with the party strife, the case of gross immorality, and the litigiousness in the Church—these were the things of which he had heard by word of mouth— and in chs. vii–xvi answering the questions which the Corinthians had put to him in their letter.

6. Before this letter was sent, it seems that Timothy had left Ephesus to go to Macedonia and Corinth,

and Paul was anxious about the reception he would have there (1 Cor. xvi. 10). (It is said in Acts xix. 22 that Timothy and Erastus were sent to Macedonia, while he stayed on at Ephesus.) At the end of his letter he announced his own intention, half hopefully, half threateningly, of going to Corinth (1 Cor. xvi. 5).

7. News came, whether through Timothy or from another source, that the situation was worse. The Apostle hurried to Corinth across the sea in order to deal with the emergency in person. (*The Painful Visit* not mentioned in Acts.) The visit was so distressing that he returned to Ephesus much troubled.

8. Conscious of his failure and of the crisis, Paul wrote a letter on his return and sent it by Titus, warning the Corinthians that he meant to come again. (2 Cor. x–xiii may be a part of this *Severe Letter*.)

9. Paul left Ephesus full of anxiety about the effect of this letter. He went to Troas, but Titus was not there. Impatiently he hurried on to Macedonia, and there met Titus, who reported the complete success of his letter. The disobedient were disowned and punished—the crisis was over.

10. The Apostle was overjoyed and wrote 2 Cor. i–ix (or perhaps the whole of 2 Corinthians) and

sent it by Titus to Corinth. (Almost certainly the Apostle visited Corinth again a short time after (Acts xx. 2).)

We thus know of four letters :

1. The Previous Letter ;
2. 1 Corinthians ;
3. The Severe Letter ;
4. 2 Corinthians ;
    and three visits :

1. When he founded the Church ;
2. A hasty visit across the sea from Ephesus and back again ;
3. After Titus had taken 2 Corinthians.

The Previous Letter. The evidence for this is 1 Cor. v. 9ff : " I wrote unto you in my epistle to have no company with fornicators ; . . . but now I write unto you not to keep company, if any man that is named a brother be a fornicator," etc. This seems clearly to imply that he had written a letter before 1 Corinthians on the subject of associating with immoral persons.[1]

The reason for thinking that a part of this Previous Letter is preserved in 2 Cor. vi. 14–vii. 1 is the change of tone in that passage, and the fact that, if

---

[1] ἔγραψα might be epistolary aorist in v. 9, but it seems unlikely, since there is nothing in the letter he is then writing to which it can refer. *v.* Lake, *The Earlier Epistles of St. Paul*, pp. 121 ff.

it is omitted, there is no appreciable break between vi. 13 and vii. 2. It is quite possible that a fragment of a letter might have been preserved in this way, but it must be remembered that we have no manuscript evidence whatever for thinking that this passage is an interpolation. A change of tone is characteristic of a letter.

1 *Corinthians*. Although this epistle treats of more subjects than any other one letter of the Apostle, it has one theme, that the foundation principle of the Christian life is love—love that should be shown first and foremost in the Christian community itself. The letter is addressed to " the church of God which is at Corinth." [1] The expression " the church of God which is at Corinth " is " laetum et ingens paradoxon," as Bengel aptly says. The Church of God in Vanity Fair.[2]

The Corinthians had learned only too well the meaning of freedom. They were keenly interested in speculation, but they did not apply their new faith to life. There were factions in the Church grouping themselves under Paul, Cephas, Apollos, Christ.[3] It seems most likely that the Cephas party claimed to be followers of the older Apostles over

---

[1] i. 2.
[2] *v.* Robertson and Plummer's *I Corinthians : International Critical Commentary*, p. xvi.
[3] i. 12.

against an upstart like Paul. The Apollos party would have claimed their intellectual superiority by their knowledge of rhetoric and philosophy. The Christ party would have been antinomian, wresting Paul's doctrine of freedom to their own uses.[1] They may have used the phrase " all things are lawful " ; it did not matter what they did with the mortal body, so long as the immortal soul sought God.

Paul reminds them that worldly wisdom is not divine wisdom, and that he and Apollos are only God's ministers. The fire itself (of the Last Day) shall prove each man's work of what sort it is (chs. i–iv).

One of the Corinthian Christians was guilty of such a sin as even the heathen world would not tolerate. The Apostle condemns him to excommunication. The evil must be purged out (ch. v).

Actually some of the Christians in Corinth were going to law with their brethren before heathen courts. Did they not know that soon Christians would be judges both of men and of angels ? (vi. 1–11).

" All things are lawful," do they say ? " But all

---

[1] Possibly there were only three parties, and ἐγὼ δὲ Χριστοῦ i. 12 is Paul's answer. v. Johannes Weiss, *Der erste Korintherbrief*, s. 15.

things are not expedient." The body is a temple of the Holy Ghost (vi. 12–20).

The rest of this letter is in answer to questions which the Corinthians had asked in their letter.

Marriage, circumcision, slavery. God's will is different for different people. Let each serve God in the calling in which he was called. In view of the nearness of the Parousia it is better not to marry (ch. vii).

Since much of the meat in the butchers' shops had come from the temples, where some part of the animal had been sacrificed, some were afraid lest in eating it they might be countenancing or even participating in idolatry. The Christian is free to eat, but he must not allow his liberty to wound the conscience of others. Christian liberty must be used in a Christian way. It is idolatry to partake of idol feasts (viii–xi. 1). The conduct of both men and women in public worship should respect universal custom (xi. 2–16).

He had heard of divisions among them even in the observance of the Lord's Supper : the rich feast, the poor go hungry. This shows a failure to realize the organic unity of all the members in Christ, with its obligation to share and help (xi. 17–34).

The Corinthians were proud of the gift of Speaking with Tongues. He reminds them that this gift does not build up the Body of Christ as intelligible preaching builds it. The unity of the Church and the service of the brethren go together. The greatest of all the Charismata is love, and all the others are worthless without it (chs. xii–xiv).

From this he passes to the Resurrection, in the light of which the life of the Christian is seen to have a share in the divine plan, only part of which is fulfilled here. The Resurrection of Christ is a fundamental fact of Apostolic preaching, of which Paul is himself a witness. Those who are Christ's share in the victory He won (ch. xv).

The last chapter is mostly about personal matters (ch. xvi).

The Painful Visit. This is not recorded in Acts, but is inferred from 2 Cor. xiii. 1–2. " This is the third time I am coming to you . . . as when I was present the second time." When he wrote that, he had already visited Corinth twice.[1] He had intended staying at Ephesus till Pentecost (1 Cor. xvi. 8), and then going to Corinth via Macedonia. But the news from Corinth made him determine to visit them twice, first from Ephesus straight across the sea, and then after going from them to Macedonia to return to them again (2 Cor. i. 15–16). He paid the former of these two visits planned but not

Cf. xii. 14, 21.

the latter, for he appears to have gone straight back from Corinth to Ephesus. Hence the charge of fickleness. This visit was so painful he could not bear another till relations were improved. " I determined this for myself, that I would not come again to you with sorrow." [1]

The Severe Letter. The evidence for this is 2 Cor. ii. 4, 9 : " Out of much affliction and anguish of heart I wrote to you with many tears." That hardly describes the First Epistle. Cf. 2 Cor. vii. 8 : " Though I made you sorry with my epistle, I do not regret it, though I did regret."

Many have thought that this letter is not wholly lost, but that a part of it at least is conserved in 2 Cor., ch. x–xiii. The arguments for this are :

1. The change of tone from chs. i–ix, which express great relief and satisfaction, to chs. x–xiii, which are written in a spirit of remonstrance, self-defence, and indignation. But it is possible to exaggerate this change of tone ; there is a minority which is still disobedient, and he is not wholly satisfied (cf. i. 17–22, v. 20, vi. 1, ix. 4).

2. In 2 Cor. xii. 20, xiii. 2 he speaks of a third visit he was shrinking from paying them : the visit is in the future. In i. 23 he seems to refer to this contemplated visit : he had not been obliged to pay

[1] ii. 1.

it. " To spare you I forbare to come unto Corinth ";
he is looking backward (cf. x. 6 with ii. 9, xiii. 10
with ii. 3).

3. He seems to commend himself in chs. x–xiii,
whereas in chs. i–ix he deprecates commending
himself.[1]   But the point is that they, the Corinthians, are his letter of commendation,[2] and it is his
opponents who arm themselves with letters of commendation, and these he attacks in chs. i–ix as well
as in x–xiii.

It is probable that the cause of his Painful Visit,
and of the Severe Letter, was the wrongdoing of
some individual, and the wrong attitude of the
Church to the offender.   Since these are not mentioned in chs. x–xiii, they cannot be more than part
of the Severe Letter.   Such a letter might not have
been preserved with much care ; perhaps the first
part was purposely suppressed.   Only later, when
the offender was dead, and everything that Paul
wrote was treasured, were all the surviving fragments of his letters collected, and it may be in
some cases combined.   But here again, as in the
Previous Letter, it is established that there was such
a letter, which comes between what we call the

[1] iii. 1, v. 12.
[2] Ye are our epistle, written in our hearts, known and read of all
men, iii. 2.

First and Second Epistles to the Corinthians, but whether either or both of these letters have, in part, been preserved within 2 Corinthians is an hypothesis which seems to many probable, but which has no manuscript evidence to support it.

2 *Corinthians*. In the first nine chapters we have the reflections of the Apostle on what must have proved one of the most distressing experiences of his life. The way in which the Corinthians dealt with the offender was a test of their loyalty to himself. He had followed his letter, in which he bade them excommunicate the wrongdoer, by a visit in which he doubtless took a strong line. Apparently a group in the Church opposed him openly, taunted him with the insignificance of his presence,[1] charged him with making promises which he did not fulfil, with arrogantly asserting authority which he did not possess. His discomfiture and failure seemed complete. On his return he wrote a letter which must have cost him much, and which might have made it impossible for him ever to visit Corinth again. No wonder that he was tortured with " without fightings, within fears "[2] until he knew what was the result of this letter. The crisis is over now, and he can express his relief.

He tells them what he had suffered and what he

[1] x. 10.   [2] vii. 5.

had learned from his suffering. He had despaired almost of life, and when he most needed it he seemed to be lacking in the affection of those whom he called his friends. But this had taught him to rely more deeply upon God. So he can write: " *We are* pressed on every side, yet not straitened ; perplexed, yet not unto despair; pursued, yet not forsaken; smitten down, yet not destroyed; always bearing about in the body the dying of Jesus, that the life also of Jesus may be manifested in our body." [1] Yet he calls this " our light affliction," and when he sees it against the background of the unseen world, he is conscious that it " worketh for us more and more exceedingly an eternal weight of glory." [2]

If there are those that charge him with the lack of those credentials which belong to a true apostle, he claims that he possesses the one thing that can give authority, the call of God in his own soul proved by the results of his ministry in the lives of men and women. They, the Corinthians, are his credentials. " Ye are our epistle . . . an epistle of Christ . . . written not with ink, but with the Spirit of the living God." [3]

The third thing on which he lays emphasis is his appeal to their generosity, that they should give " not grudgingly or of necessity " but bountifully,

[1] iv. 8–10.   [2] iv. 17.   [3] iii 2, 3.

to the needs of the poor among the Christians in Jerusalem. It was good for those who were at strife with one another in Corinth to look farther afield to the needs of the Church outside. The climax of his appeal is the example of Christ, " who though he was rich, yet for your sakes he became poor, that ye through his poverty might become rich." [1]

This letter, with its alternation of subjects, corresponding to the swift changes of mood of the writer, is a very human document. R. H. Strachan says " it is an artless and unconsciously autobiographical description of the ways in which Paul was accustomed to meet slander and calumny, physical danger and bodily suffering, disloyalty and ingratitude, from those for whom he had given of his best, the disillusionment and disappointment that invaded his spirit from time to time." [2]

If chs. x–xiii are a genuine part of the letter, and are not part of the Severe Letter, then we must assume that, having expressed his relief at the news which Titus brought him, he turns to those who still formed the unruly minority at the end, asserting his authority in self-defence, and denouncing his opponents with words of stern rebuke and warning.

[1] viii. 9.
[2] *The Moffatt N.T. Commentary—2 Corinthians*, p. xxix.

CHAPTER IV

THE EPISTLE TO THE GALATIANS

Causes of Writing and Significance of the Issue.
" The Epistle to the Galatians is not a theological treatise ; it is a religious appeal." [1]   It is the passionate outpouring of the Apostle's soul in vindication of the Gospel, which he has been commissioned to preach, and of the faith, which has made all things new for himself.   It is a letter and not a treatise, but the writer is so intensely affected by the circumstances which compel him to write, that he neglects some of the more formal characteristics of a letter.   He does not associate anyone else with himself in the opening salutation ; he has no thanksgiving, as in all his other letters, and while at the end he takes the pen [2] from the amanuensis a little earlier than usual, he adds no personal greetings.

Paul writes in his own name only, because his letter is an *apologia pro vita sua.* The Galatian Christians, most of whom were Gentiles, seem eagerly and hastily to have embraced the suggestion that they should be circumcised and become

[1] G. S. Duncan, *The Moffatt N.T. Commentary—Galatians*, p. xxxiv.
[2] vi. 11.

practising Jews. This was not Paul's Gospel, and if his converts were accepting it, it could only be because some other teachers were denying his authority and claiming that he was only a second-class apostle. He vehemently asserts that his authority was not of human origin, nor through human agency,[1] but "through revelation of Jesus Christ."[2] He recounts the occasions on which he came into touch with the apostles in Jerusalem, and how they taught him nothing but recognized his apostleship to the Gentiles.[3] His independence is shown by the fact that he withstood Peter face to face at Antioch when he, with Barnabas, was carried away by the dissimulation of certain brethren from Jerusalem.[4] The question at issue was whether Jew and Gentile could eat together because they were both Christians. The action of Peter in withdrawing from table fellowship with Gentiles split the unity of the fellowship of Christ. Paul quotes his argument with Peter, and from that develops his case on the wider issue which is at stake among these Galatian converts. The question is not merely one of how Gentile and Jewish Christians are to live together, but it is the fundamental question, " What is Christianity ? " Is it faith in Christ, or obedience to the Jewish Law ?

[1] i. 1.   [2] i. 12.   [3] i. 18 ff., ii. 1 ff.   [4] ii. 11 ff.

There is no doubt that many good Jews who had embraced Christianity were shocked by teaching which denied the fundamental principles of Judaism. For them the will of God and the Law of God were the same thing. God's demand was that men should obey His word, that is, the Jewish Law. Israel had received that Law to pass it on to the nations. Jesus had said that He came to fulfil the Law[1] : the Gospel was the fulfilment of the Law. Therefore the Gentiles must accept the Law as the command of God, and so gain a place in the covenant which God had made with Abraham. To observe the Law was the way to become a more perfect Christian. The thing to be wondered at is that Paul, himself a Jew, saw so clearly the issue, that the Gospel supersedes the Law, and that it is faith, not the Law, which is the means of salvation. What led him to contend so sharply against the Law was his own experience. The Law could not bring men to God; indeed, the Law is an afterthought in the working-out of the divine purpose. It is no positive aid to righteousness, it puts men under condemnation and a curse. The Law is our slave attendant. It held us as wards in discipline, a discipline which was to last till Christ came.[2] Under the Gospel we are sons of God. Man needs

[1] Matt. v. 17.   [2] iii. 24. παιδαγωγὸς ; ; ; εἰς Χριστόν,

deliverance from the condemnation of the Law. When the time had fully come " God sent forth his Son, born of a woman, born under the Law, to ransom those who were under the Law, that we might get our sonship." [1] Our Deliverer died a death pronounced accursed by the Law. But God raised Jesus from the dead, therefore the curse of the Law no longer holds : therefore He has power to rescue men from the curse of the Law. The Crucifixion of the Messiah made invalid the Jewish Law as a system. The Gentiles are free from any obligation to accept the Law. " The just shall live by faith "—the just, whether he be Jew or Gentile. Christ died for our redemption, and we are summoned to have faith in One who thus gave Himself for us. On the basis of that faith God accepts us, forgiving our sins and imparting to us His Holy Spirit.

It has been suggested that those who were disturbing the Galatian converts were the local Jews in the Churches, who were eager to draw the Gentiles into the synagogue, and who were jealous of Paul's success in winning those whom they would gladly have attached to Judaism. But more likely they were Jewish Christians from Jerusalem like those mentioned in Acts xv. 1, who thought to keep

---

[1] iv. 4, 5 (Moffatt).

Christianity within the framework of Judaism. The whole future of Christianity was at stake in Paul's emphatic refusal to let Christianity be bound up with the Law. As a reformed Judaism, Christianity would have been no gospel.

Destination. In the third century B.C. a tribe of Gauls had settled in Asia Minor, and when Rome conquered the East, they retained the status of an independent kingdom. Augustus included this kingdom of the Galatae in the Roman province of Galatia, which in the south embraced parts of the old geographical divisions Lycaonia, Pisidia, and Phrygia. Are the Galatians to whom Paul wrote this epistle to be understood ethnographically or politically ? Were they the descendants of the Gauls in the northern part of the province, whose chief cities were Ancyra,[1] Pessinus, and Tavium ; or were they the Christians in (Pisidian) Antioch, Iconium, Lystra, and Derbe—the cities which Paul had evangelized on his first missionary journey in the south of the Roman province ? [2]

Lightfoot's arguments [3] in favour of the northern theory are :

1. In popular use " Galatae " means the Gauls in the north of the province.

---

[1] The modern Angora, the seat of the Turkish Government.
[2] Acts xiii. 14—xiv. 23.   [3] In his commentary on the Epistle.

2. In Acts Antioch is called Pisidian, Lystra and Derbe cities of Lycaonia, not Galatian. The inhabitants of these cities in the south would not have called themselves Galatians because that term reminded them of their subjection to Rome.

3. The words τὴν Φρυγίαν καὶ Γαλατικὴν χώραν (the region of Phrygia and Galatia, R.V.) in Acts xvi. 6 and τὴν Γαλατικὴν χώραν καὶ Φρυγίαν (the region of Galatia and Phrygia, R.V.) in Acts xviii. 23 both mean the same district, so called because it was land once occupied by Phrygians and now by Gauls, or land which was partly Galatian and partly Phrygian.

4. Mysia, Phrygia, Pisidia are all geographical, not political, terms in Acts : therefore Galatia is not politically used. Acts does not use the name Galatia at all on the first journey when Paul went to Antioch, etc.

5. The fickle character of the Galatians to which the epistle bears witness is consistent with their Gallic origin.[1]

6. This theory suits the date of the epistle—on the third journey—a little before Romans.

The arguments for the southern theory which Ramsay has strenuously affirmed are :

1. The more probable meaning of the phrase in

[1] i. 6, iii. 1.

Acts xvi. 6 is the " Phrygio-Galatic region," i.e.
that part of Phrygia which was in the province of
Galatia. The words in Acts xviii. 23 mean " the
Galatic region and Phrygia," i.e. districts in the
province of Galatia, and that part of Phrygia which
was in the province of Asia.

Apart from these two passages of which the
interpretation may be doubtful, Acts nowhere gives
any account of missionary activity in the north of
the province.

2. The northern kingdom of the Galatae was
hardly opened up enough for Paul's opponents to
have gone there after him : through the cities in
the south of the province there was a constant
stream of commerce. Was Paul likely to have gone
up to this rougher northern country when sick ?
In Gal. iv. 13 he says " because of an infirmity of
the flesh I preached to you originally (or formerly)." [1]
This suits the occasion when he fell ill at Perga and
went up to the high ground of Pisidian Antioch on
his first journey.[2]

3. Barnabas is mentioned in Gal. ii. 1 as if he
was well known to the readers : but he accompanied Paul only on the first journey,[3] i.e. to the
cities in the south of the province.

4. The Galatians took part in the collection for

[1] τὸ πρότερον, R.V. " the first time." [2] Acts xiii. 14. [3] Cf. Acts xv. 39.

the poor, but sent no delegates to Jerusalem with it, unless Gaius and Timothy were delegates, and they came from Derbe and Lystra (Acts xx. 4).

5. Perhaps " you received me as a messenger of God "[1] is a reference to the scene at Lystra when Paul was taken for Hermes ; and the " marks of the Lord Jesus " might be a reference to the stoning at Lystra.[2]

6. The people in the south of the province, though not Galatians by race, but only politically, would not have resented being called Galatians, which was the only comprehensive title to embrace the citizens of all the cities—Antioch, Iconium, Lystra, and Derbe. Paul was not ashamed of being a Roman citizen.[3]

The southern theory grows in favour, but no one who accepts it will deny that the northern theory is at least arguable, and many English and Continental scholars still adhere to it.

Date and Place of Writing. 1. Since Paul in recounting his relation with those who had been " apostles before him " mentions two visits to Jerusalem (Gal. i. 18, ii. 1), it is natural to assume those are the two visits mentioned in Acts ix. 26 and

---

[1] Gal. iv. 14 ; Acts xiv. 12.   [2] Gal. vi. 17 ; Acts xiv. 19.
[3] Acts xxii. 28.

Acts xi. 30. The first is after his conversion, and although Acts implies it was soon after, whereas in Gal. i. 18 he says it was three years after, there can be little doubt that they refer to the same event. The difficulty is to know whether the second visit fourteen years later (Gal. ii. 1) is to be identified with the second visit in Acts xi. 27-30, in which it is said that Barnabas and Saul took up the collection for those suffering from the famine. In Gal. ii. 2 Paul says he went up " by revelation," and that might refer to the fact that Agabus had prophesied the famine. It would seem unlikely that when the Apostle is recalling his connexion with the elders at Jerusalem he would deliberately omit the mention of a visit there, even if it had nothing to do with the matter. But in Gal. ii. 2 ff. it appears that on this occasion he discussed his Gentile mission with the Apostles. This rather accords with the visit to the Council at Jerusalem (Acts xv), when the question of the circumcision of the Gentile Christians was the point at issue.

If the second visit in Gal. ii. 1 is the " famine-visit " (Acts xi. 27-30), then the epistle might have been written before the Council at Jerusalem, and will be the earliest of the Pauline letters we possess. This assumes that the south Galatian theory is true, and it explains why the Apostle did not mention the decrees of the Council in his letter. The decrees were not yet in existence.

If the second visit in Gal. ii. 1 is the visit to the Council (Acts xv), then there remains the difficulty of explaining why he omitted to mention the " famine-visit " (Acts xi. 27-30). Lightfoot thinks he omitted it because it was not relevant. Rénan suggested—and Streeter [1] inclines to accept—that perhaps there is a slight mistake in Acts xi. 30. Barnabas and another took the collection : the author of Acts wrongly assumed the other was Barnabas's travelling companion Saul. Lake [2] thinks that Acts xi. 27-30 and Acts xv. 4 refer to the same event ; the former comes from an Antiochian source and the latter from a Jerusalem source, so that we have two descriptions of the same visit.

That would mean that Galatians was written sometime after the Council. This suits both the south and north Galatian theories.

2. In Gal. iv. 13 Paul says " because of an infirmity of the flesh I preached the gospel to you the first time." τὸ πρότερον in classical Greek means the " former of two," and would imply he had preached already twice to them before he wrote. But in Hellenistic Greek it often means "originally,"

---

[1] *The Four Gospels*, p. 557, note.
[2] *The Beginnings of Christianity*, vol. v, pp. 195-204.

"formerly"; and this is its meaning elsewhere in the New Testament.[1]   Therefore it gives no certain clue of date.

3. Galatians in style and thought seems to belong to the group of epistles 1 and 2 Corinthians and Romans.   If they were written on the third journey, presumably Galatians was written about the same time.   But it cannot be denied that if the original Romans was a circular letter, afterwards adapted for the Roman Church, then both Galatians and this original Romans might have been written before the Council.   It seems, however, very improbable that, after writing two such letters, Paul should have written a year or two later 1 and 2 Thessalonians, in which he does not seem to have reached maturity as a writer of letters.   If, on the other hand, there was no earlier draft of Romans, and the epistle as we have it was written on the third journey, whereas Galatians had been written some years previously before the Council, then we must suppose the Judaistic controversy had broken out again, so that he felt it necessary to renew the arguments he had previously used.

Agreement is not likely to be reached on this debatable point.

Some scholars who accept the south Galatian

[1] Tim. i. 13 ; Heb. iv. 6.

destination date the epistle before the Council, after Paul had returned from the first journey from Antioch, or on the way up to Jerusalem to the Council. But many others favour a later date from Macedonia or Corinth on the second journey, or (and this is more likely) on the third journey during the stay at Ephesus [1] or at Corinth or on the journey between the two.[2] If the readers lived in north Galatia, the epistle must be later than Acts xvi. 6, which refers to the second journey, and is probably later than Acts xviii. 23, the beginning of the third journey.

Why did not Paul quote the decrees of the Apostolic Council, if he wrote after that had settled the question of the admission of the Gentiles? According to Acts xvi. 4, he had already published them in the cities of southern Galatia. And was it not more in accordance with Paul's practice to convince his readers by argument, rather than to appeal to authority, especially in an epistle where he so vigorously claims his independence? [3]

It has been urged that the epistle must have been written before the Council because Peter would not have dissembled, as he did,[4] after the Council had

---

[1] As in the Marcionite Prologue to the Epistle, scribens eis ab Epheso.
[2] Acts xx. 1–3.
[3] v. F. C. Burkitt, *Christian Beginnings*, p. 122.
[4] Gal. ii. 11 ff.

passed regulations for the intercourse of Gentile
and Jewish Christians. But it may be that that
refers to an incident earlier in date than the previous
verses (Gal. ii. 1–10), or perhaps there is some confusion in Acts. The Council settled that the
Gentile believers need not be circumcised. Later,
perhaps, another Council laid down regulations for
the social intercourse of Jew and Gentile.[1] The
author of Acts has telescoped the two into one,
whereas it was the difficulty which Peter and others
felt, which afterwards caused these decrees to be
adopted. If this is so, then while Paul played an
important part in the first Council about circumcision, he may not have had anything to do with
the minimum-law requirement for the regulation of
social intercourse until his last visit to Jerusalem
(Acts xxi. 15), when James seems to have mentioned
the decrees to him as a new thing of which he was
unaware.

Genuineness. This is unquestioned in the early
Church. Marcion included it in his Canon; so
does the Muratorian Fragment. Even the Tübingen school did not doubt it : F. C. Baur based his
reconstruction of the history of the early Church
upon it.

[1] *v.* Foakes Jackson and Lake, *The Beginnings of Christianity*, vol. **v**,
pp. 210 ff.

CHAPTER V

THE EPISTLE TO THE ROMANS

Purpose. If it is asked why Paul wrote this letter
to the Romans, the answer is in his own words that
he writes " to impart to them some spiritual gift "
(i. 11, xv. 15). He does not here insist on his
authority as an Apostle, but he writes partly to take
the place of a visit, partly to prepare them for such a
visit. If he warns against errors,[1] it is probably
because he knows from experience such errors were
found in apostolic Christianity generally. He
writes to ask for their support to help him on his
proposed visit to Spain.[2] Ramsay thinks Paul had
conceived the idea of an imperial Church organized
on a world-wide basis. But surely he thought of
the Church as a body rather than an empire; and,
while not neglectful of organization, it was not of
paramount importance to him because of his belief
in the Advent. But he deliberately planted Christianity in the strategic positions in great centres of
population. Therefore it was natural that he
should give expression to his conclusions about the
whole history of God's manifestation of Himself in

[1] Rom. xvi. 17 ff.   [2] xv. 24, 28.

a letter addressed to the Church in the centre of the world.   And if ch. xvi belonged originally to the letter, then he knew many Christians there intimately, and so he can give that personal touch to his writing which makes it a letter and not a treatise ; and he can assume the foundations of the Christian creed and deal with the problems of its development.   Therefore, when he discusses predestination and the rejection of Israel, it is not in an academic way, but as one who loved his nation with a passion that belonged to his inmost nature.[1]   It is one of the ironies of history that so sincere a patriot should have been pursued with implacable hostility by his fellow-countrymen from city to city, and finally deprived of liberty and life, because he saw a vision of a world-wide commonwealth of God, in which there should be neither Jew nor Gentile—and because he was " not disobedient to the heavenly vision." [2]

Theme. The theme which Paul set forth in Galatians is the theme of Romans. But in the shorter letter he wrote at fever heat : the crisis was so significant, he poured out his soul in an impassioned plea for the freedom of the Gospel over against Jewish legalism. In Romans he explains, at greater length and in a wider context, the thoughts

---

[1] Cf. ix. 3.   [2] Acts xxvi. 19.

which in Galatians were rough-hewn. The theme is the ultimate basis of soteriology—the answer to the question " What is Christianity ? "

Both Gentile and Jew have failed to attain righteousness, but God has made it possible for all, Gentile and Jew, if they have faith in Jesus Christ to stand right with Him. Sin, since it is an offence against divine law, means that mankind are in a status of guilt. The redemption which was won by Christ, thought of in this legal sense, means a verdict of acquittal, i.e. a new status : justification. But sin is like a disease; when it awakes in a man, life becomes death. The redemption which Christ brings is that by Baptism we are so united with Him we die to sin, and rise to a new life.[1] The law of the spirit of life which is in Christ emancipates us from the law of sin and death.[2] We have the Spirit of Christ, and so we can live the life of the Spirit : sanctification. But to Paul, who had for so long waged a losing battle against sin,[3] the peace which he now experienced, however described—justification or sanctification—was God's doing, the result of God's favour which man had not earned, but which every man, Jew or Gentile, could experience through faith. Then, if faith itself, by which alone this redemption can be experienced, is a gift of God,

[1] vi. 4.   [2] viii. 2.   [3] vii. 15 ff.

why is it given to some and not to others ? Why is
Israel rejected ? The answer [1] lies in the absolute
sovereignty of God, which surpasses man's powers
of understanding, and in the ultimate purpose of
mercy for all. So from justification he passes to
sanctification, and so to predestination, because of
the rejection of the Chosen People, the heirs of the
promise, which was one of the most baffling problems before the early Church.

Date. If ch. xvi is part of the epistle, then it
seems likely that Corinth was the place of origin ;
for Phoebe, " deaconess of Cenchreae," the port of
Corinth, takes it [2] : Paul is staying with Gaius [3] :
Erastus, Timothy, and Sopater are mentioned, and
these were with him in Greece (Acts xix. 22, xx. 4).
The Apostle describes his plans in ch. xv : he hopes
to go to Rome, but is now going to Jerusalem with
the collection for the saints (Acts xix. 21). He had
already visited Illyricum, [4] presumably on his third
journey. He does not seem to have gone there on
his second journey, where we have a detailed
account of the places visited.

Sometime between A.D. 57 and 59 is the probable
date for this letter. It was the quinquennium of
Nero, when the brightest hopes were entertained for
the future. The provinces were well governed,

[1] In chs. ix-xi.   [2] xvi. 1.   [3] xvi. 23.   [4] xv. 19.

and trade was flourishing. The hostility of the imperial power to the Church was still in the future; and the Apostle to the Gentiles could lay down his laws for the respect due to the authorities (ch. xiii), with sincere thankfulness for the real benefits which the world at large, and the interests of law and order, received at the hands of the Empire.

The Church in Rome. It is not known how the Church in Rome was founded. The Emperor Claudius banished the Jews from Rome in A.D. 49— Suetonius [1] says because they kept rioting at the instigation of Chrestus. This may refer to trouble arising in the synagogue, when Christianity was preached in Rome. (But edicts against the Jews had been issued before Christian times.)

Aquila and Priscilla were probably Christians when Paul met them in Corinth,[2] where they had arrived on being banished by this edict. It may be assumed that Christianity had found its way to Rome before A.D. 49. The Roman tradition says Peter founded the Church, but the earliest form of it makes Peter and Paul joint founders. This is contradicted by Romans, and it is very unlikely Peter had ever been to Rome before 49. Most likely the

---

[1] *Claudius*, ch. xxv. Iudaeos impulsore Chresto assidue tumultuantes Roma expulit. Suetonius may have confused Christus with the Greek name Χρηστός. Perhaps Paul has this edict in mind in writing xiii. 1 ff.

[2] Acts xviii. 2.

two Apostles were martyred in Rome. But the
Church was founded through the extraordinary
facilities for travel and intercourse in the Empire in
this century. There was a continual current of
commerce and public affairs in the direction of
Rome; and it is not unlikely that friends or converts of Paul were among the earliest Christians in
Rome. Perhaps the description of Mary, "who
bestowed much labour upon you,"[1] and of
Andronicus and Junias,[2] "my kinsmen, and my
fellow-prisoners, who are of note among the
apostles, who also have been in Christ before
me," may signify that they had taken a special part
in founding the Church.

The Church was clearly Greek-speaking, as we
should expect. It would have numbered among
its members freedmen, slaves, artisans, tradesmen.
Narcissus[3] may be the freedman of Claudius; and
Aristobulus[4] may be the grandson of Herod; to
the members of whose households the Apostle
sends greeting. The writings of the Church
in Rome for the first two Christian centuries
are in Greek. The names in ch. xvi, like
the earliest names in the catacombs, are mostly
Greek.

When the Neronian persecution broke out, the

[1] xvi. 6.   xvi. 7.   xvi. 11.   xvi. 10.

Christians in Rome were a large body.[1] Tacitus says "an immense multitude." It may well be that the Church was large enough at that time to be represented as a public danger, and was numerous and influential, when Paul addressed this letter to it.

It is almost certain that such a Church would have been of Jewish origin and Gentile growth. This is supported by the letter Paul wrote to it. In certain passages he has Gentile readers in mind— " that I might have some fruit in you also, even as in the rest of the Gentiles." [2] " I speak to you that are Gentiles." [3] In others he associates himself with his readers as Jews—" Abraham *our* forefather according to the flesh." [4] His argument presupposes knowledge of the Old Testament. It is implied that the relation of Jew and Gentile in the Church is a matter of vital interest to the readers, though not a burning question, as it was when he wrote Galatians ; nor is it to be inferred that the Judaistic teaching had gained a strong footing in Rome.

Integrity. Were chs. xv and xvi a part of the original epistle ? The question arises because :

1. Some MSS. omit ' in Rome ' in i. 7, 15.

2. The Doxology (xvi. 25–27) is found in some MSS. at the end of ch. xvi only ; in others at the

----

[1] πολὺ πλῆθος ἐκλεκτῶν, 1 Clement vi. 1.   [2] i. 13.
[3] xi. 13.   [4] iv. 1, cf. vii. 6, ix. 10.

end of ch. xiv only; in others in both places; in P⁴⁶ it is found after xv. 33; in others it is omitted altogether, as it is in Marcion.

3. Marcion seems to have had the epistle without chs. xv and xvi, and some MSS. of the Vulgate seem originally to have had only fourteen chapters.

4. Some MSS. read the benediction after xvi. 20; others after xvi. 20 and xvi. 24; others after xvi. 27.

5. Some modern scholars think ch. xvi was a fragment of a letter to Ephesus for the following reasons:

(*a*) It contains many greetings to individuals in a Church to which the writer was a stranger. Would Paul have known so many in Rome, and would he have been so closely associated with them as is implied in xvi. 7, 13?

(*b*) Aquila and Priscilla were in Ephesus (Acts xviii. 19; 1 Cor. xvi. 19). Between the writing of 1 Corinthians and this epistle they must have settled in Rome again, and yet they were back in Ephesus, according to 2 Tim. iv. 19, when Paul was in prison in Rome.

(*c*) The tone of the warnings in Rom. xvi. 17–20 is not consistent with what we know of the Roman Church from chs. i to xv: it rather suggests the sort of false teachers whom Paul refuted in writing Colossians.

(*d*) Ch. xvi reads like a letter of commendation of Phoebe, which would be more natural to a Church which the Apostle knew well and where he had some authority.

(*e*) The reference to Epaenetus, "the firstfruits of Asia,"[1] would have more point if he were writing to the chief city of Asia.

(*f*) The words of xv. 33 read like the conclusion of a letter. "Now the God of peace be with you all. Amen." In P[46] these words are followed by the Doxology (xvi. 25–27).

(*g*) It is to be noted that in the Captivity Epistles, if they were written from Rome, no one of those saluted in ch. xvi is mentioned. (This might equally be used as an argument against the Ephesian origin of the Captivity Epistles.)

On the other hand, there is no evidence in the MSS. for separating this chapter from ch. xv. Even in P[46], in which the Doxology (xvi. 25–27) appears at the end of ch. xv, the opening words of ch. xvi follow in the same line. Further, it was not Paul's custom to send personal greetings to the members of a Church he knew well, where greetings might make invidious distinctions; but he might well wish to establish as many individual contacts as possible at Rome. And the words of xv. 33, as the

[1] xvi. 5.

conclusion of a letter, are unlike the conclusions of all his other letters. Moreover, the names can almost all be paralleled from the catacombs and inscriptions. Nor is there clear evidence that the warning against dissensions and false teaching in xvi. 17–20 was not equally as suitable for Rome as for Ephesus.

It can hardly be said that the case for separating ch. xvi as a part of another letter is proved, though it has no lack of advocates.

But the problem of the last two chapters remains. Two explanations are offered :

1. The original epistle consisted of fourteen chapters written as a circular letter about the same time as he wrote Galatians. He used this later for Rome, adding the last two chapters as a sort of " covering letter " (Lake).[1] The difficulty is that the thought continues after ch. xiv until xv. 13. Burkitt thinks that while xiv. 23 was the conclusion of his argument, xv. 1–13 is just such an addition as a man would make when adapting something already written for a new purpose.[2] But it seems strange that the warm expressions in i. 8–13, " how unceasingly I make mention of you in my prayers," etc., were written for others, and that the Roman

[1] *The Earlier Epistles of St. Paul*, pp. 324 ff.
[2] *Christian Beginnings*, p. 127.

Christians were reading expressions of personal desire to see them which had originally been written without a thought of them.

2. The other explanation is that the original epistle had sixteen chapters, and that the Apostle shortened it for use as a circular letter. The evidence of P[46], which inserts the Doxology after xv. 33, points rather to a xv chapter edition for liturgical reasons—ch. xvi not being regarded as suitable for public reading—than to ch. xvi as part of a separate letter to another church. Perhaps Marcion, taking exception for doctrinal reasons to the references to the Jews in ch. xv,[1] made a still shorter edition of xiv chapters only. Some confusion may have arisen between these two shorter editions. Possibly a copy of the epistle suffered mutilation in some persecution in Rome, and so a shorter edition became current, which was adopted by Marcion and seems to have been known to Origen. If the Doxology (xvi. 25–27) was not from the Apostle, it might have been added to the Corpus Paulinum, when Romans was placed last of his epistles to Churches, as in the Muratorian Fragment.[2]

Canonicity. There are reasons for thinking that

---

[1] Especially to the description of Christ, διάκονος περιτομῆς, xv. 8.

[2] It must not be forgotten that although we speak of " the break at

the writers of 1 Peter, Hebrews, the Epistle of James, the Epistle of Jude have all been influenced by Romans.[1]

Clement of Rome refers to Romans several times. Ignatius and Polycarp show identity of thought. Marcion includes it, in the shorter recension, in his Canon. It is mentioned in the Muratorian Fragment. From Irenaeus onwards there are many direct quotations. Even the Tübingen school did not doubt its genuineness, although Baur rejected the last two chapters, since to call Christ a " minister of circumcision " (xv. 8) was inconsistent with his idea of Pauline doctrine.

the end of ch. xiv," and so on, the division into chapters was not known until Stephen Langton invented it at the beginning of the thirteenth century; and that the division into verses was first used in the edition of the Greek Testament by Robert Stephanus in 1551.

[1] 1 Pet. ii. 6, 8, 10; Rom. ix. 26, 32, 33: 1 Pet. ii. 13–17; Rom. xiii. 1–7: Heb. xi. 11, 12, 19; Rom. iv. 17–21: Jas. ii. 14–26; Rom. iii. 28, iv, 1–62; Jude 24, 25; Rom. xvi. 25–27.

CHAPTER VI

THE CAPTIVITY EPISTLES

Time and Place of Writing. The group of letters to the Philippians, to the Colossians, to Philemon, to the Ephesians, were all written when Paul was a prisoner. In the narrative of Acts three imprisonments of Paul are mentioned—at Philippi,[1] where clearly he had no opportunity to write letters ; at Caesarea,[2] where he was kept in prison for two years ; at Rome, where, when Acts closes, he had been in prison for two years.[3] Tradition has assigned these four letters to his imprisonment in Rome.

The Evidence for Rome as the Place of Writing. 1. We know from Acts and from universal tradition that Paul was for two years a prisoner in Rome, and since we have a group of letters which belong to his travels, and these letters, especially Colossians and Ephesians (written when a prisoner [4]), differ in style and subject-matter from the letters of that group, it seems reasonable to suppose that these were written from Rome at a later period in his

---

[1] xvi. 23.   [2] xxiii. 23.   [3] xxviii. 30.
[4] Col. iv. 3, 18 ; Eph. iii. 1, iv. 1, vi. 20.

life. Since he was a prisoner when he wrote Philippians,[1] it seems equally reasonable to suppose that it was written during the same two years.

2. Clearly Rome is more probable than Caesarea as the place of writing of these letters if we are to group them together. (It is not quite clear that we are right to group them as all belonging to one period : *v. infra*, p. 77 ff.) A runaway slave, Onesimus, would not be likely to find his way to Caesarea —but he might to Rome—much as fugitives from justice seek to hide themselves in London.

3. In these letters Paul mentions a number of companions who are with him. Besides Onesimus, Timothy, Epaphras, Mark, Jesus Justus, Aristarchus, Demas, and Luke, are with him when he writes Colossians. Tychicus takes the letter and Aristarchus is described as " my fellow-prisoner." [2] Aristarchus [3] of Thessalonica started with Paul on the voyage to Rome, though it is not said that he was a prisoner. Only Aristarchus, Mark, and Jesus Justus appear to have been Jews,[4] and that fact suggests he is in Rome rather than in Caesarea, where many of his friends would have been Jews. Tychicus takes the Ephesian letter.[5] The same group of friends join in the greetings of the letter to Philemon as in

---

[1] Phil. i. 7, 13, 17. [2] Col. iv. 10. [3] Acts xxvii. 2.
[4] Col. iv. 10–11. [5] Eph. vi. 21.

the letter to the Colossians. In Philemon, he writes:
"Prepare me also a lodging: for I hope that through
your prayers I shall be granted unto you."[1] That
hardly suits Caesarea—for he knew that since he had
appealed to Caesar, he must go to Rome before he
could visit any of his friends in Asia again. Similarly,
in writing to the Philippians, he says he hopes soon
to visit them.[2] That cannot, for the same reason,
have been written from Caesarea. Timothy joins
in the salutation to the Philippians, so if the others
are from Rome, there is a presumption Philippians
is.[3] But both of these arguments are rather against
Caesarea than in favour of Rome.

4. Phil. i. 12. "The things *which happened*
unto me have fallen out rather unto the progress of
the gospel; so that my bonds became manifest in
Christ in the whole Praetorium[4]—and to all the
rest." "The Praetorium" in the Gospels and Acts
is the Roman Governor's palace in Jerusalem[5] and
Caesarea. But it was also used for the Praetorian
guard, the Emperor's bodyguard, the headquarters
of which were in Rome. The difficulty is that they
numbered 9,000, and it hardly seems likely Paul's
bonds were known among all these. Mommsen

---

[1] Philem. 22.   [2] Phil. ii. 24.   [3] Phil. i. 1.
[4] R. V. margin: ἐν ὅλῳ τῷ πραιτωρίῳ.
[5] Mark xv, 16; John xviii, 28, etc.; Acts xxiii. 35.

N.T.—4

suggested that it means the Praetorii Praefecti—the court before whom Paul was tried in Rome. If so, then the trial has already begun. Both these interpretations are possible.

5. Phil. iv. 22. " All the saints salute you, especially they that are of Caesar's household." This might well refer to Christians among the slaves and others who were members of the Emperor's extensive entourage.

If then we have to decide between Caesarea or Rome as the place of writing these letters, everything points to Rome. There is little or nothing to support, but many points which tell against Caesarea—not least that if Paul had written from there, would he not have sent greetings from Philip, in whose house he stayed on his way up to Jerusalem ?[1] His friends were allowed to visit him.[2]

The Evidence for Ephesus as the Place of Writing. About thirty years ago H. Lisco, of Berlin, put forward the hypothesis that Paul had been imprisoned during his stay of three years at Ephesus, and that during this imprisonment he wrote these Captivity Epistles. This hypothesis received little attention at the time, but Deissmann, who had already suggested it independently, was sympathetic; and it

---

[1] Acts xxi. 8. [2] Acts xxiv. 23.

has won the support of a number of other Continental and English scholars during the last ten years.[1]

The most important arguments in support of the belief that the Apostle suffered imprisonment or imprisonments in Ephesus are :

1. In 2 Cor. xi. 23 Paul claims that in comparison with his enemies at Corinth he has been in prison far more frequently. This passage, if part of the Severe Letter to Corinth, was written from Ephesus ; or, if part of 2 Corinthians, was written from Macedonia after leaving Ephesus. The difference of date is only a few months and does not matter. Up to this point Acts has only recorded one imprisonment, that at Philippi,[2] so that the narrative in Acts is obviously incomplete.

2. In 1 Cor. xv. 30–32 Paul writes, " if after the manner of men I fought with beasts at Ephesus, what doth it profit me ? " This suggests, if the words are understood in their literal sense, that at Ephesus Paul had been exposed in the arena. This may be what he refers to in 1 Cor. iv. 9 : " God means us apostles to come in at the very end, like the doomed gladiators in the arena." (Moffatt.)

3. 2 Cor. i. 8–10. " For we would not have you

[1] G. S. Duncan, v. St. Paul's Ephesian Ministry.
[2] Acts xvi. 23.

ignorant, brethren, concerning our affliction which befell *us* in Asia, that we were weighed down exceedingly, beyond our power, insomuch that we despaired even of life : yea, we ourselves have had the answer of death within ourselves, that we should not trust in ourselves, but in God which raiseth the dead : who delivered us out of so great a death, and will deliver." He seems to refer to some desperate danger from which he had been supernaturally saved.

4. In Rom. xvi. 3, Priscilla and Aquila are described as having " risked their necks for my life," and in xvi. 7 Andronicus and Junias are called " my fellow-prisoners." This might be a reference to the same danger which befell him in Ephesus. Otherwise we do not know to what it refers.

5. Later tradition, which dates back at least to the early part of the third century, relates that Paul was thrown to a lion in the arena at Ephesus, and that the lion licked his feet.[1] (The story sounds apocryphal, and, while it may be based on fact, it may go back to nothing more than Paul's own words : " If I fought with beasts at Ephesus " (1 Cor. xv. 32).)

6. In Ephesus is still shown a building traditionally known as Paul's prison.

[1] The evidence is given by G. S. Duncan, *op. cit.*, pp. 69 ff.

7. In what is called the Marcionite Prologue to Colossians it is written—" the apostle when bound wrote to them from Ephesus." This is thought to go back to the second century, and probably to Marcion.

If Paul suffered imprisonment in Ephesus, why is it not mentioned in Acts ? One answer is, that, if Luke wrote Acts as a defence of Christianity which might help Paul at his trial, he may have deliberately avoided mentioning such an incident, because it would have brought in the name of the proconsul of Asia—Silanus—who would in some measure have been responsible for his imprisonment or for his release. This Silanus had been put to death by Agrippina because he was more popular than Nero. It was politic to omit any reference to his name.

But if Acts was written some years after Paul's death, we cannot say why Luke omitted the story of the Ephesian imprisonment. It is clear, however, that since Paul in 2 Cor. xi. 23 hints at many imprisonments, Luke must have omitted other such events in other cities.

Whether Paul fought with beasts literally or only metaphorically in Ephesus, there is nothing inherently improbable in the supposition that he was imprisoned in Ephesus during some part of the three years he was there. It is not merely possible—it is indeed probable—from his references to the danger

that beset him in Asia.[1]   If so, it is quite possible
that he wrote letters during this imprisonment.

The reasons for thinking that these Captivity
Epistles were written during an imprisonment in
Ephesus are :

1. Onesimus was more likely to flee from Colossae, where his master, Philemon, lived, to Ephesus
than to Rome, and he might quite well have met
there Epaphras, a Colossian, who arranged for him
to meet Paul. It was about 800 miles from Colossae
to Rome.

2. In Philem. 22 Paul says : " Withal prepare me
also a lodging : for I hope that through your prayers
I shall be granted unto you." Clearly he hoped soon
to visit Colossae, so that it was quite safe for him
to tell Philemon that he would pay whatever sum
Onesimus had stolen from him.[2]   Was this likely
when Paul was in Rome, so far away ? Especially
when we remember that his plan had been, according
to Rom. xv. 28, to go to Spain from Rome ; and
although he came to Rome as a prisoner, if he were
released, we should expect he would seek to carry
out this plan rather than go back to the East.

3. Would not Paul have been more likely to
write to Colossae, a Church he had not yet visited,
before he went to Rome, when he was in the same

[1] 2 Cor. i. 8 ff.   [2] Philem. 18, 19.

province—assuming that the Church had come into being there as the result of his influence while in Ephesus? [1] These considerations suggest that Philemon and Colossians might have been written from Ephesus, assuming Paul did suffer imprisonment there. Ephesians so-called, if a genuine epistle of Paul, has no personal notes to guide us, except that Tychicus takes it, who takes Colossians. In subject-matter it is so closely akin to Colossians that it is natural to assume they were written about the same time and from the same place.

But, on the other hand, when Paul wrote Philemon and Colossians, Luke was with him—among others. We have no reason to believe that the others mentioned may not have been with him at Ephesus: Timothy was there (Acts xix. 22). But we know Luke was with Paul in Rome from the closing chapters of Acts: we do not know that Luke was with him in Ephesus. The inference is from Acts that Luke was not there, because Acts xix is not a " We-section," and, apart from the riot, the description of the three years there is meagre. Besides, it would be easier to account for Luke's silence about Paul's imprisonment, if he was not present in Ephesus at the time. This is a strong argument in favour of Rome as the place where Philemon and

[1] Acts xix. 10.

Colossians were written : Ephesians also, if genuine, will have been written about the same time and from the same place. The Marcionite prologue to the epistle supports this, and so does the term " Paul—πρεσβύτης, the aged " [1]—which the Apostle uses of himself in Philem. 9. We do not know how old he was, but not more than middle-aged at the period of his greatest activity as a traveller. If these epistles are from Rome, they will have been written some six or seven years later than if they had been written from Ephesus.

When these four Captivity Epistles are considered together, Ephesians and Colossians are clearly akin in style and subject-matter : Philemon is a private letter, but is associated with Colossians in destination. Philippians stands apart from the others : in style and thought it is much more like the letters to the Corinthians and to the Romans than like the Ephesian and Colossian letters. So much so that, if Rome be the place of origin of the four, then either Philippians was written soon after Paul arrived there, and the other letters near the end of his two years' imprisonment, as Lightfoot suggested; or the other way round, Colossians and Ephesians were written soon after he arrived in Rome, and Philippians nearly two years later. It seems neces-

---

[1] The word might mean ambassador, πρεσβευτής, as in LXX.

sary to imagine an interval between the writing of Philippians and of Colossians. This suggests the possibility of assigning Philippians to the earlier group of letters, with which it has more affinities. If so, it might have been written from Ephesus, supposing that Paul was a prisoner there.

The arguments are as follows :

1. According to Phil. iv. 16 the Philippians had sent once and again to his need when he was in Thessalonica—that is, shortly after the imprisonment in Philippi. According to 2 Cor. xi. 9 the brethren, when they came from Macedonia, "supplied the measure of my want," i.e. Timothy and Silas brought him a present from Macedonia— probably from Philippi when they rejoined Paul at Corinth. When he writes to the Philippians he thanks them for their gift and says they lacked opportunity of reviving their thought of him before (Phil. iv. 10). If this is written from Ephesus, it is some months, or two or three years, after they had sent to him in Corinth. But if he is writing from Rome, it is ten years or so since they sent to him : and it seems strange they had had no opportunity to send to him in so long a time. And during that time he had passed through Philippi twice (Acts xx. 1, 3, 6).

2. In Phil. ii. 19 Paul hoped to send Timothy to

Philippi : he sent him in Acts xix. 22 from Ephesus. Paul expects to follow soon after (Phil. ii. 24). Timothy accompanied him on the third journey, but did not accompany him to Rome, so far as we know (cf. Acts xix. 21, 1 Cor. xvi. 5).

3. There seem to have been frequent communications between Philippi and Paul's place of imprisonment. Epaphroditus had brought him their gift, and had fallen ill (Phil. ii. 25, 27, iv. 18) : news of his illness had reached Philippi (ii. 26). Such communications would seem scarcely possible if Paul was in Rome several hundred miles away from Philippi, but would be much more likely if he was writing from Ephesus.

4. Phil. i. 13 and iv. 22 could apply to Ephesus equally well as to Rome. " My bonds became manifest in Christ in the whole Praetorium" (i. 13). The Praetorium was the Roman Governor's official residence, as in Matt. xxvii. 27 in Jerusalem, and in Acts xxiii. 35 in Caesarea; the addition of the phrase " and to all the rest " implies that the Praetorium means the people rather than the building; he is well known to all who have taken part in his examination and to all the rest of the governor's suite : or it might refer to Praetoriani in Ephesus— a small company of the Praetorian guard on some imperial errand.

5. Phil. iv. 22, " The saints of Caesar's household." Caesar had members of his household in every part of the world, a sort of Civil Service managing his affairs : they formed themselves into collegia or guilds, and we have one or two inscriptions which speak of such in Ephesus itself.

6. Since Luke's presence with Paul is an argument for Rome as the place of writing of Colossians and Philemon—for Luke was his companion on the voyage to Rome—so the absence of Luke's name in the greetings to the Philippians suggests that it was written from a place where Luke was not with him, and this seems to have been true of Ephesus.

7. There is one point which seems to favour Rome. In i. 20–24 he speaks of his hope that Christ " shall be magnified in my body, whether by life or death "—as if he were awaiting the decision of a trial, and it might mean death. Cf. ii. 17, " I am poured out as a drink-offering upon the sacrifice and service of your faith." If he is really fearing the death penalty, he must be in Rome, for in any provincial city he could avert the death sentence by an appeal to Rome (cf. Acts xvi. 37, xxii. 25–29, xxv. 10–12). But it is not quite clear that the danger to which his life was exposed was the issue of a judicial trial : he speaks of many perils in 2 Cor. xi. 26, " in perils from my countrymen, in perils

from the Gentiles, in perils in the city—in perils among false brethren " : just above is the phrase " in deaths oft " (v. 23). These words were written probably when he was in Ephesus ; and the verses quoted from Philippians might be a reference to the same circumstances.

The traditional order of the epistles, however, is supported by signs of change and development in Paul's thought—particularly in his eschatology. In 1 Corinthians the present life is strictly provisional—" the time is short " ; human institutions have no positive value. In the Captivity Epistles the imminence of the Advent has fallen into the background, and the present life has gained in significance. Family life receives Paul's blessing in Colossians ; in Ephesians the marriage relationship, " which in 1 Corinthians was regarded as irrelevant to the Christian life, is made the vehicle of the highest conceivable spiritual values." [1] Philippians seems to express the latest form of Paul's psychological development. It is there " that we see most clearly what experience has made of this naturally proud, self-assertive, and impatient man." [2] The balance of evidence therefore supports Rome, the traditional place of writing of the Captivity Epistles.

[1] C. H. Dodd, *The Mind of Paul : Change and Development* (*Bulletin of the John Rylands Library*, vol. 18, No. 1).

[2] *The Mind of Paul : a Psychological Approach* (*Bulletin*, vol. 17, No. 1).

CHAPTER VII

THE EPISTLE TO THE COLOSSIANS

Colossae was a city in the valley of the Lycus, a large and fertile plain which lies in the heart of Asia Minor about 100 miles east of Ephesus. Paul had heard of the " faith in Christ Jesus " and of the " love in the Spirit " of the Christians there (i. 4, 8). This implies he did not know them personally : indeed, he says as much in ii. 1, " I would have you know how greatly I strive for you, and for them at Laodicea, and for as many as have not seen my face in the flesh." He had not been to Colossae or Laodicea. Epaphras probably founded the Church (i. 7, 8). We may presume that the Church at Colossae was founded during Paul's three years' residence in Ephesus, when, according to Acts xix. 10, " all they which dwelt in Asia " (the Roman province) " heard the word of the Lord, both Jews and Greeks."

Cause of Writing.—We have already seen reason to believe that Paul was a prisoner in Rome when he wrote this letter. He had heard news from Epaphras, and probably from Onesimus, the runaway slave, who also came from Colossae, that caused him to write this letter to Colossae, and another to the Church at Laodicea, and he wished the letters to be interchanged (iv. 16). Paul evidently knew Philemon well, or he would not have written to him as he wrote about Onesimus : and since Colossae and the other Churches were doubtless the fruit of his own work in Ephesus, he has a peculiar interest in them. We may suppose that the letter was written as the result of what Epaphras had told him; and he had spoken in warm terms of the faith and hope and love of his fellow-Christians in his native town; but he had also told Paul of certain strange doctrines which were gaining ground, and which he himself had found it difficult to answer. Epaphras may well have asked the Apostle to write this letter, and since Paul may have known something of the dangers to which the Christians in Colossae were exposed from false teaching, by his own experience at Ephesus, he feels it is important enough to devote a letter almost wholly to its refutation. At the end he deals with another subject— not related to the heresy—but one which was much in his mind because of his interest in Onesimus, the slave of the Colossian, Philemon. He takes occasion to express his thoughts about the whole matter of domestic relations, the duties of husbands, wives, children and parents, masters and slaves.

The Colossian Heresy.   We have no knowledge of the particular form of false teaching which was prevalent at Colossae except from Paul's letter, and it is not likely to have been Essenism[1] or Cerinthianism.   It was a religious system probably composed out of pagan mythology and speculative philosophy, and it had some elements in it borrowed from Judaism.   This may seem strange— the combination of paganism with Judaism—but there were large numbers of Jews living in the Lycus valley; and these teachers may have borrowed Jewish elements, or have been themselves Jews in birth and upbringing.   At any rate, they taught that the Colossian Christians should observe festivals, the Sabbath, new moons, and so on,[2] and should avoid certain foods as unclean.   In addition, they stressed certain mystic rites and asceticism :   they required that the Colossians should worship angels ;[3] they called their teaching a theosophy or philosophy, and claimed that the Christianity which Epaphras had taught was only a preliminary step to a deeper, vaster, and humbler philosophy.   Theirs was the completion of Christianity.

At the back of this false teaching is the dualism of matter and spirit—evil and good—which is clearly taught in the religion of Persia, and which

[1] As Lightfoot supposed.   [2] ii. 16.   [3] ii. 18.

profoundly influenced religious thought in this and succeeding ages.

Evil was of two kinds : moral, and from that Christ is the deliverer ; material—man is a creature of the earth : his spiritual nature is hampered by great cosmical forces : so by asceticism man must free himself from the pollution of matter : by mysterious rites he must counter the forces of evil. And further, he must gain to his side the supernatural beings who belong to the realm of the spirit, and who will protect him from the supernatural beings who belong to the material, i.e. evil, world. Therefore he needs not only faith in Christ, but the help of angels—the fulness of the Godhead is brought into relationship with men by angels who must be worshipped. (" Let no man rob you of your prize . . . by worship of angels " (ii. 18).)

It may be this particular form of false teaching was only prevalent at Colossae and in its neighbourhood, but it was similar in idea to the Gnosticism of a later period, and Paul indicated the way to meet it.

Paul's Refutation. For Paul the religions of the world were not upon a level, so that each had its contribution to the final religion, which is in some sense a synthesis of all. Christ was not one power out of many—He is absolutely pre-eminent. He is

the very secret of the life of the universe of which
we are a part, the very principle by which all things
cohere, the very actuality of the divine in human
life. There is a mystery, but these false teachers
have not been initiated into it : it is the Person of
Christ, who is the " image of the invisible God."
He is supreme over angels—for they owe their
existence to him—thrones, dominions, principalities,
and powers, all things have been created by Him and
unto Him—He is supreme over the Church—that
He may be pre-eminent in all things.[1]   In this Paul
sets forth a view of the Person of Christ, which is
like that in the prologue of the Fourth Gospel : he
does not expressly call Christ the Logos, but he
speaks of Him in terms which imply that it is
through Christ that God has effected His work of
creation.   In Christ we must seek for the ultimate
meaning of the world : all else exists for those
spiritual ends, which were supremely manifested
in His life and teaching : apart from Him and that
for which He stands the universe loses its meaning.

More than that : Christ is not only the source
of universal life—He is the source of that life which
is operative in the Church.   And the Church is the
beginning of a world-wide process of reconciliation.
(This is worked out in Ephesians.)   Why should

i. 15–23.

the Colossians worship angels along with Christ, when it is clear that in Christ dwelt a divine power which made Him different from all created beings?

According to the false teachers the divine nature had many aspects or energies (aeons). These powers taken all together were the πλήρωμα, the totality or fulness of the Godhead. The false teachers said God was in some measure in Christ, but Christ was only one aspect of the divine nature, and in Himself not sufficient. Paul replies " in him the divine Fulness willed to settle without limit."[1] " Christ is the centre and the whole circle of all the things that are."

So it is not by Jewish circumcision that the Colossians can be perfected, but by spiritual circumcision, which is given in baptism when the believer is united with Christ. And as Christ died, so the believer at baptism goes into the water and dies to the old life. As Christ rose again, so the believer, united with Him, rises in triumph with Him. For on the Cross God cancelled the charges against us and triumphed over the angelic powers which were hostile to man (ii. 11–15).

The Colossians were warned not to trust to human ordinances of food and drink and festivals— " let no one disqualify you because you have not

i. 19 (Moffatt).

advanced in the so-called higher instruction "—
but hold fast to Christ Who is the Head from
Whom the whole body receives its life.[1]   You died
with Christ to the angelic powers that belong to the
material world, you have been raised with Christ—
therefore aim at what is above where Christ is.
When Christ appears, then you will appear with
Him in your true character, since your life is one
with His.[2]

The Message of the Epistle.   We no longer think
of supernatural powers from which we need pro-
tection.   But " we still think of ourselves as held
in bondage by iron forces, inexorable laws of
heredity and environment in the face of which all
our aspirations are futile."   The message of this
epistle is that " through Christ we can reach out
beyond the hostility of all material forces, to a life
of spiritual freedom.   We have a power on our
side, which can overcome everything that is
against us." [3]

The Epistle from Laodicea.[4]   This seems to mean
a letter which the Apostle had written to Laodicea
and sent at the same time as this letter to the Colossians.   In several MSS. of 1 Timothy, the words
are found, " it was written from Laodicea."   But

---

[1] ii. 17-19.   [2] iii. 1-4.
[3] E. F. Scott, *Moffatt N.T. Commentary*, p. 50.
[4] iv. 16, τὴν ἐκ Λαοδικίας.

Paul had not been to Laodicea (Col. ii. 1). Marcion placed Ephesians in his Canon under the title πρὸς Λαοδικέας (to the Laodiceans).[1] If that is a mistake, then the letter to the Laodiceans must be reckoned among those many writings of the primitive Church which have not survived. A so-called Epistle to the Laodiceans is found in Latin in a number of MSS. It is quite short, and seems to be made up of phrases from the genuine epistles pieced together. " It is quite harmless," says Lightfoot, " so far as falsity and stupidity combined can ever be regarded as harmless." [2]

Genuineness. There are apparent echoes of this epistle in Barnabas, Clement of Rome, Ignatius, and Justin. Marcion included it in his Canon, which seems to confirm its acceptance at Rome. It is cited by Irenaeus, Tertullian, Clement of Alexandria, and is named in the Muratorian Fragment.

The Tübingen school attacked it on the ground that (*a*) its ideas are not those of the four genuine

---

[1] W. F. Howard has suggested to me that since in Apoc. chs. ii and iii the Seven Churches begin with Ephesus and end with Laodicea, if Paul, when writing to Colossae, is referring to our " Ephesians " (an encyclical letter), it would be at that point the " letter from Laodicea," and so the letter to Colossae would have been read there in exchange.

[2] Lightfoot thinks this apocryphal epistle is a translation from a Greek original. Possibly it was known to the author of the Muratorian Fragment, who mentions two letters, one to the Laodiceans and another to the Alexandrians, forged in the name of Paul. *v.* Lightfoot, *The Epistle to the Colossians*, pp. 281–300.

epistles ; (*b*) it seeks to refute the Gnosticism of the second century, and therefore must be many years later than Paul. But the first objection is based upon far too rigid and narrow a view of Paul's mind ; and the second is not true. It may be granted that the style and vocabulary differ appreciably from the earlier epistles. On the other hand, many of his characteristic words and phrases occur here. The subject and circumstances are not those with which he has dealt hitherto—nor are they such as to call for the rather personal argumentative methods of the Corinthian and Galatian epistles. The Christology is more advanced in the sense that what was implicit in 1 Cor. viii. 6 is developed in Col. i. 15 ff. Similarly, in 1 Cor. ii. 6 ff. the triumph of the Redeemer over the hostile spirits is only mentioned incidentally : here it is further developed because it is central to his argument (Col. ii. 15). The Gnosticism of the second century was no sudden growth. For a long time a syncretism of religions had been taking place, and the germs of it were found quite as early as Paul's time in many quarters where Greek, Jewish, and Oriental systems of thought had opportunities of meeting, as in Asia Minor.

CHAPTER VIII

THE EPISTLE TO PHILEMON

Genuineness. This epistle was included by Marcion among the ten epistles in his " apostolicon." It is mentioned in the Muratorian Fragment. In all the early lists it was included among the epistles of Paul. And although quotations from it are rare, that is to be expected because of its untheological character. No serious doubt has been felt about its genuineness, except by those who have questioned the Pauline authorship of all but the four epistles of the Travel-group. No one is likely to have composed such a letter in the name of the Apostle, and the Church is hardly likely to have kept such a letter, unless it had been written by an Apostle.

Purpose. The letter to Philemon is unique among the correspondence of Paul which has come down to us. It is a letter to a friend on a very delicate personal matter. Onesimus had always been to Philemon an unsatisfactory servant ; and finally he had run away—apparently with a sum of money belonging to his master.[1] He had found his way

[1] v. 18.

to Rome, and there perhaps had been recognized by
Epaphras and brought to Paul. Or in his lone-
liness he may have sought Paul in prison, so that
Paul would like to have kept him. But that was
not right ; Onesimus must return. Paul writes to
ask Philemon to forgive his slave. He does not
ask him to release him. Paul accepted slavery as
part of the social order and requires slaves to submit to their lot and be faithful to their masters in
Christ.[1] He avoids any direct criticism of social
and political institutions : he would have effected
nothing by attacking them, and would have caused
his mission to be suspected as revolutionary. Besides, Paul is convinced that the present order of
things is quickly coming to an end, and the one
thing necessary was to make sure of his calling as
a Christian, whether a man was a slave or free.
" Let every man, wherein he is called, therein
abide with God " (1 Cor. vii. 24).   Philemon
is not bidden to release Onesimus, but to
love him—a far harder thing. Thus the sting
of slavery was withdrawn, and the principle laid
down which in the end led to the abolition of
slavery.

The letter, short though it is, gives insight into
the character of the Apostle, showing his warm

[1] Cf. Col. iii. 22.

affection for the slave, now a brother in Christ, and his delicate tact towards the master.

Time and Place. Paul is in prison as when he wrote Colossians, i.e. in Rome. Probably Philemon lived in Colossae, for Onesimus is described as accompanying Tychicus thither and as " one of you," i.e. a Colossian (Col. iv. 9).

CHAPTER IX

THE EPISTLE TO THE EPHESIANS

Destination. To whom was this epistle addressed? The question arises because in the first verse the place name (to those who are) " in Ephesus " is wanting in our oldest and most trustworthy MSS. And the epistle makes it clear that the writer does not know the readers personally. " I have heard of the faith in the Lord Jesus Christ which is among you " [1]—" if you have heard of the dispensation of that grace of God which was given me to you Gentiles." [2] Surely the Christians in Ephesus had both heard and seen that grace in Paul's three years among them. We may be sure that the epistle was not originally written to Ephesus—and that is all of which we can be sure. Perhaps Paul wrote this as a circular letter to be read by Tychicus in some of the Churches through which he would pass on his way to Colossae; perhaps it was written originally to Laodicea. Marcion entitled it the " letter to the Laodiceans," and we know from Col. iv. 16 that Paul wrote an epistle to the Laodiceans. Harnack suggested that, if it

[1] i. 15. [2] iii. 2.

was written to Laodicea, there is a reason why the name should have been lost. Laodicea was in disgrace when the writer of the Apocalypse wrote[1]; it was the black sheep of his scathing description, and no one cared to associate it with this noble epistle, so that the name was omitted. But neither of these explanations is quite convincing. It may well be that a copy of the epistle, for some cause we have not yet guessed, was known without a name; and at Ephesus, where perhaps the first collection of Paul's letters was made, the name (to the saints who are) " in Ephesus " was added, because it was felt to be fitting that Paul should have written at least one letter to so important a Church.

Genuineness. In the case both of Colossians and of Ephesians doubts have been raised as to their genuineness on the ground that in style, vocabulary, and doctrine, they differ from the earlier epistles of the Travel-group, which are undoubtedly genuine. In the case of Colossians it seems sufficient to note that the circumstances which called it forth are different, and that the doctrine of the Person of Christ does not contradict that of the earlier epistles, but develops certain thoughts hinted at there.

The case against the genuineness of Ephesians appears to many scholars to be much stronger.

[1] Apoc. iii. 14 ff.

1. There are more than seventy words and phrases not found elsewhere in Paul. But this may be discounted if it belongs to a later period in his life.

2. It is closely related to Colossians, of which it is called "a catholicized version."[1] Would Paul have copied from himself? But it is not a mere copy of the ideas of Colossians; it is a development, e.g. in the doctrine of the Church as the body of Christ in its mystical significance. Is it not more likely that Paul himself used the phrases and thoughts which he had already expressed and developed them, rather than that another imitating him developed them thus? An imitator trying to pass this off as Paul's would have stuck more closely to his model.

3. It is asked whether Paul would have used the phrase " holy apostles and prophets " (iii. 5), when he claimed to be one himself. But the word "holy" is the word translated " saints," i.e. Christians : he had used it of the Corinthians [2]—he might surely have used it of himself : originally it meant " consecrated." And again, may not Paul have sincerely called himself " less than the least of all saints,"[3]

---

[1] Moffatt, *Introduction to the New Testament*, p. 393.

[2] κλητοῖς ἁγίοις, 1 Cor. i. 2.

[3] ἐμοὶ τῷ ἐλαχιστοτέρῳ πάντων ἁγίων, iii. 8.

remembering, as he always did, what he had been before the vision on the road to Damascus?

4. The style is different from that in most of his letters. Moffatt[1] says: "In Paul's letters there is always something of the cascade: in Ephesians we have a slow, bright stream which brims its high banks." In plain prose it means that here we have a few interminable sentences, in which the clauses become tangled with each other. But the first three chapters are almost a prayer: he is not here a spiritual father eager to correct his converts, nor is he a fiery combatant replying to attacks—he is contemplating the mystery of God's purpose for the world, and his style befits his high mood of contemplation. It is difficult to believe that an imitator could have produced a work so like the writings of Paul and yet so splendid and original: difficult to believe some other spiritual genius was to be found in the Church at this time whose mind was so like Paul's and whose thought was so sublime.

5. There are traces of the use of Ephesians perhaps in Clement of Rome, more certainly in Ignatius, Polycarp, and Hermas. Marcion included it in his Canon.[2] It is mentioned in the Muratorian Fragment. Irenaeus quotes it by name,

---

[1] *Introduction to the New Testament*, p. 389.
[2] But called it the "Epistle to the Laodiceans."

and there is no hint of any doubt about it in the early Church.

6. There are affinities between Ephesians and Acts, particularly in Paul's address to the Ephesian elders at Miletus,[1] but that may support the trustworthiness of Luke's summary of the address, rather than cast doubt upon the genuineness of Ephesians. There are affinities in language with 1 Peter,[2] and in thought with the Fourth Gospel and Hebrews. But if the author of 1 Peter was influenced by Romans, he may also have been by Ephesians. And many of those who deny its Pauline authorship date it not later than A.D. 75–85.

Purpose and Place of Writing. Paul wrote Colossians because he was afraid lest the Christians of Colossae, in whom he was much interested, might be led astray by the false and dangerous doctrines which were being preached among them. In his discussion of this false teaching he was led to certain new ideas which were obviously of far-reaching significance, and he sets himself in Ephesians to explain them further on their positive rather than on their controversial side, and to show their practical bearing. It may be that his experience

---

[1] Acts xx. 18 ff., a " We-section."
[2] Eph. iv. 9, cf. 1 Pet. iii. 19, iv. 6 ; Eph. iv. 18, cf. 1 Pet. i. 14 ; Eph. vi. 10 ff., cf. 1 Pet v. 8, 9.

of the Roman empire in its vigour, its strength, and its vast serviceableness had made him think of the Church as that by which unity and coherence could be won for the life of man, a unity which would not make Jew and Gentile merely members of the same empire, but which would break down the bitter hatred between them. The Church was to be more than that; it was to be the means of giving harmony to the whole universe. It is not necessary to suppose that Paul was in Rome when this great thought was worked out by him in a letter, but it is quite consistent with the supposition that he was there, where, though a prisoner, he was conscious of the throb of the life of the world's metropolis all around him. He is a prisoner (iii. 1, iv. 1, vi. 20), and there is no reason to doubt that he wrote this from the prison from which he wrote Colossians.

The Theme. The epistle falls into two clearly marked sections—in chs. i.–iii he dwells on the Christian message and the divine purpose of God for the universe. In chs. iv–vi he is concerned with the duties required of Christians as members of the Body of Christ. All Paul's letters follow the forms customary at that time. Ancient letters began with some pious formula thanking the gods for the reader's well-being. Paul begins with thanksgiving in Christian language.[1] But the introductory prayer here lasts for three chapters, and that explains the sustained elevation of style. It is not argument; it is prayer.

His theme is the mystery of God's purpose—God " having made known unto us the mystery of His will, . . . to sum up all things in Christ, the things in the heavens and the things upon the earth " (i. 9 ff). The divine purpose is the ultimate union of all things in Christ. The universe has suffered some disaster, has become divided against itself. There are unreconciled powers confronting the sovereignty of God. A conflict has arisen in heavenly places which has caused all the antagonisms that we find in nature, in human society, in ourselves. God's purpose is to reconcile all things to Himself and to do it through Christ. That has always been God's purpose ; now it is a mystery revealed. The proof that it is so is the creation of a society in which already we see Jew and Gentile reconciled and united—the Church. The enmity of Jew and Gentile was the bitterest in the ancient world : the unity of Jew and Gentile was the most signal manifestation of reconciling grace. The symbol of the division between Jew and Gentile was the Law. The curse of the Law fell on Christ, and the

[1] i. 3 ff.

Christian, whether Jew or Gentile, was accursed from the Law with Christ. On the Cross Christ "brake down the middle wall of partition"[1] dividing Jew and Gentile, and enabled them to enter on a new life in which the old differences were transcended. When a man is in Christ he is no longer Jew or Gentile, he is a new man.[2] As Jew or Gentile he is dead, as a Christian he is God's handiwork.[3]

Jew and Gentile are united, not primarily with one another, but with God, and therefore with one another. On this basis a human society can be built up, which is in its very nature a unity, as God Himself is one.

But more than this—God's purpose is to achieve unity, harmony in the universe, and here the Church is to be His instrument. We are aware of the discord in the universe. Paul refuses to believe it can be permanent. This is God's world, He created it that material and spiritual should serve His purpose. Paul thinks of the discord as due to rebellious angels—principalities and powers in the heavenly places—such as had compassed Christ's death : these had been conquered by Christ, who won the victory over them in His resurrection. They are now to learn the divine purpose through the Church.[4]

---

[1] ii. 14.   [2] ii. 15.   [3] ii. 10, αὐτοῦ ποίημα.   [4] iii. 10.

In the world of Paul, Jew and Gentile lived together, but the Pax Romana did not reconcile the bitter enmity between them. In the modern world nations, which dislike, suspect, and fear each other, have learned that by some amount of mutual concessions they can at least for a time live together without war. But peace can only be established if the nations can be drawn into a true community of mankind. That means that the nations submit to be controlled by ideals which are not divisive, but are large enough to be common to them all. Paul's idea of the Church is of a society in which the discordant elements of human life are harmonized, the instrument for reconciling all things to God.

We do not believe in the supernatural powers of evil which were in the air men breathed. Christ's victory over them is proved by nothing more decisively than by the fact that men have ceased to believe in their existence.[1] But men feel themselves in the grip of a vast mechanism and of inexorable laws of physics and the like, and human freedom seems to have no meaning in face of cosmic forces. We learn from this epistle to believe that all these but subserve a spiritual purpose, and that spiritual purpose is summed up in Christ.

It is more difficult to follow Paul when he thinks

[1] T. R. Glover, *Jesus in the Experience of Men*, ch. i.

that the Church will achieve harmony in the universe. It has not yet reconciled men, and in any case, how could it affect the cosmos? E. F. Scott [1] answers: " a new departure in creation, a wonderful experiment is in process here, and who can foresee where it is destined to end? Is it not possible that influences are taking shape on earth which are destined in some way to affect the universe? If this is so, there is surely some profound significance in the Church, the institution which stands for man's higher life, and seeks to manifest and unfold it. It is not presumptuous to believe that issues are bound up with the Church which are far vaster than we know."

The second part of the epistle is the practical issue of the purpose of God worked out in a man's common life. The Church stands for a new humanity, and that will show itself in the development of the Christian character in its members. Christians are servants of Christ, their duty is to co-operate with Him in the work of reconciliation. All their actions in the home and the Church and the world must be directed to love, peace, mutual understanding. Each of them is to be a centre of reconciliation, as Christ is to the world. And in order to carry out this task the followers of Christ are to hold fast to

---

[1] The Epistles of Paul, *Moffatt N.T. Commentary*, p. 134.

Him like members of the body which draws vitality from the head.   As they fulfil the law of Christ in the home, the Church, the society around them, they are co-operating with God in His eternal purpose for the world.   This is implicit in the Apostle's words to wives, husbands, children, servants, and masters.[1]

Last of all, he reminds his readers the Christian life is always a struggle.   Christ has indeed put the powers of evil under His feet, but for the Christian there are still enemies to be encountered.   The conflicts in which he is involved are part of the process through which the universe is being brought into the unity and peace of the kingdom of God. He must therefore fight like a good soldier of Jesus Christ, and he has been given weapons for the battle.[2]

[1] v. 22 ff.   [2] vi. 10–20.

CHAPTER X

THE EPISTLE TO THE PHILIPPIANS

Occasion of Writing. Paul is a prisoner, possibly at Ephesus, possibly at Rome.[1] Philippi was the first Church which he had founded in Europe. There is a special bond between the Apostle and the Philippians. He calls them " my brethren beloved and longed for, my joy and crown " (iv. 1). They were the symbol of his victory, the sure proof that he had not run in vain. He would have them recognize that the things which had happened to him— he seems to mean his imprisonment—had made for the advance rather than the hindrance of the Gospel (i. 12–18). He tells them he is sending Timothy and hopes to come himself to visit them (ii. 24).

But there were two reasons for his writing this letter: (1) Epaphroditus had brought him a gift of money, and he wishes to thank his friends.[2] He writes " to all the saints in Christ Jesus which are at Philippi, with the bishops and deacons." [3] Nowhere else does he address the officials of the Church. Possibly the officials had sent the gift by Epaphroditus. Their messenger had been so

[1] *v. supra,* ch. vi.   [2] iv. 10 ff.   [3] i. 1.

zealous in his service to the Apostle that he had
broken down, and now that he was better Paul
decided to send him back to Philippi. The
Philippians, he knew, were willing for their representative to stay with the Apostle as long as he
was needed, and Paul, to prevent them thinking
that Epaphroditus was deserting him, sends this
affectionate letter, in which he calls him "my brother
and fellow-worker and fellow-soldier." [1]

It seems not unlikely that he had written earlier
to acknowledge their gift, or he would have referred
to it before the end of his letter. Perhaps in some
way his letter had been misunderstood, and he
administers a gentle reproof as he insists on his
independence.[2] (2) He is obliged to write to them
because of things which are not right in the Church.
He exhorts them to be united among themselves in
the face of pagan opposition and misrepresentation
(i. 27–30); and to put aside party spirit and vain-
glory (ii. 3), treating one another with the same
spirit which they had experienced in Christ, Who
emptied Himself and received the name that is
above every name (ii. 5–11).

It does not seem that there were parties in the
Philippian as in the Corinthian Church : there was
no division caused by false teachers, and no moral

---

[1] ii. 25–30.   [2] iv. 11–18.

laxity as at Corinth; but there were murmurings
and disputings, and there were two women in particular who were the cause of friction in the Church,
Euodia and Syntyche (iv. 2). There is an absence
of severity in the Apostle's censure, except in iii.
1b–iv. 1, a passage which raises the question of the
unity of the epistle.

Unity. The passage beginning iii. 1b is different
in tone from the rest of the letter, and seems to refer
to a danger of more serious kind. No one doubts
that it was written by Paul, who here becomes again
a fiery combatant as in Galatians. Two explanations are offered. He may have been interrupted
at this point, as Lightfoot suggested; and before
returning to the letter he was angered by hearing
of some fresh activity on the part of his Judaizing
opponents in the city where he was a prisoner,
Ephesus or Rome, and he was afraid for his beloved
Philippian converts. Or this may be a fragment of
another letter combined with the present, when a
collection of Pauline letters was made. In favour
of the former view (*a*) there is no manuscript evidence for any break at this point; and (*b*) those who
think it is a fragment of another letter are not agreed
as to where the interpolation ends. Michael[1] thinks

[1] The Philippian Interpolation, where does it end? *Expositor*, Jan.
1910.

the intruding passage ends at iii. 19, others at iv. 1 (McNeile),[1] others at iv. 3 (Lake).[2] But in considering whether this passage may be a fragment of another letter, it must be acknowledged that it is not unlikely that Paul wrote other letters to Philippi. Polycarp, in writing to the Philippians, refers to Paul who " when he was absent wrote letters to you " (καὶ ἀπὼν ὑμῖν ἔγραψεν ἐπιστολάς).[3] Lightfoot, however, claims that the plural ἐπιστολαί was used of a letter of importance.

Message. Bengel says " summa epistolae, gaudeo, gaudete." The theme is the joy of the Christian. The Philippians are not exhorted to rejoice, because of the happiness of their circumstances, seeing that they were the objects of persecution. The ground of their joy is the fellowship in the Gospel. Philippi enjoyed as a military colony the Roman franchise. The pride of its citizens is reflected in Acts xvi. 20, 21: " These men are proclaiming customs which as Romans we are not allowed to accept or observe." Paul reminds them that they are a " colony of heaven " [4]—their names are enrolled as burgesses there, and " we wait for a Saviour from there, the

---

[1] *Introduction to the New Testament*, p. 168.

[2] Critical Problems of the Epistle to the Philippians, *Expositor*, June 1914.

[3] Ad Philipp. iii. 2.

[4] So Moffatt translates τὸ πολίτευμα ἐν οὐρανοῖς.

Lord Jesus Christ" (iii. 20). Five times the near return of the Lord is mentioned, by which we may be assured that the ultimate *dénouement* of history will be brought about by that divine power which has been already witnessed in the Resurrection of Christ. And the secret of Christian joy is fellowship, not with one another, but with the risen and glorified Christ. It is joy in the Lord, and to know Christ as Lord is the one thing of transcendent value (iii. 8). Christ was given " the name that is above every name " because He went the way of love and self-sacrifice. This love is the supreme power in the universe and will supply every need (iv. 19).

Date. 1. If the epistle was written from Ephesus, it would have been during the three years which the Apostle spent there on this third journey (Acts xix). If 1 Cor. xv. 32 (" if I fought with beasts at Ephesus ") refers to an imprisonment, then this letter would have been written before 1 Corinthians. Otherwise it may have been written between 1 and 2 Corinthians.

2. If it was written from Rome, it is not quite clear whether it was the first or the last of the Captivity group. Lightfoot thinks it was the first because of the affinity in language and thought with Romans, and the differences in language and

thought between Philippians and Colossians and Ephesians.

But most scholars who think the epistle was written from Rome date it last of the four, on the ground that (a) time must be allowed for the Apostle's bonds to have become known " in the whole Praetorium," whether it means the Praetorian guard or the Court. In the latter case it implies that the trial has already begun ; and his " defence of the Gospel " will mean his self-defence at the trial ; and " the salvation " for which he hopes will mean acquittal (Ramsay). (b) Time is needed for communications between Philippi and Rome; for the Philippians to have sent a contribution to the Apostle ; for Epaphroditus to have fallen ill; for the Philippians to have heard of his illness ; and for the Apostle to have heard that they had received the news.

Canonicity. There are traces of the epistle in Clement of Rome, Ignatius, and Polycarp. Marcion included it in his Canon ; the Muratorian Fragment has it among the Pauline Epistles. From Irenaeus onwards the evidence is clear and decisive. No serious doubt has been entertained about its genuineness except by the Tübingen school.

CHAPTER XI

THE PASTORAL EPISTLES

Thomas Aquinas seems to have used this name of the two letters to Timothy, but Paul Anton, in 1726, used it of the three letters, and it has now gained universal currency.   In our early MSS. and lists of New Testament books these letters were grouped with Philemon as private letters to personal friends ; but they were soon separated from Philemon, as of less personal nature and as of value for Church life.   And as long ago as the second century some who accepted Philemon rejected these letters.[1]   The name Pastoral is not altogether suitable, but it is convenient.

The epistles present four problems.

1. *The Personal Allusions*.   The historical situation presupposed by these letters as they stand seems to be this :

In 1 Timothy Paul has lately left Ephesus to go to Macedonia (i. 3), but he hopes to return to Ephesus shortly (iii. 14).   There is no hint that he is a prisoner.   On the contrary, iii. 14 and iv. 13 suggest he is not a prisoner.

[1] Marcion rejected them all. Tatian apparently rejected 1 and 2 Timothy.

In Titus Paul has left Titus in Crete (i. 5). He has apparently gone to the mainland, for he bids Titus come to him at Nicopolis (in Epirus), where he will winter (iii. 12). Here, too, it is implied Paul is not a prisoner.

In 2 Tim. i. 8, Paul is a prisoner (cf. i. 15–18, from which it may be inferred he is a prisoner in Rome). He has lately been at Troas and Miletus (iv. 13, 20). He is awaiting the day of execution (iv. 6–8).

It is inferred that Paul, after his two years' imprisonment in Acts xxviii, was released; that he had a further period of missionary activity in the East, in Ephesus, Crete and Greece; and that he was arrested again, and wrote 2 Timothy when he was about to be martyred. We cannot reconstruct his movements with any certainty; nor do we know why he was arrested or where; nor on what charge he was to be executed.

In support of this it is said that Acts ends on a note of optimism. " Be it known therefore unto you that this salvation of God is sent unto the Gentiles : they will also hear." And then follow the verses which describe him dwelling in his own house, preaching the kingdom and none forbidding him (Acts xxviii. 28–31). It seems as if we are to infer that at the end of the two years something happened—release—acquittal. If Phil. ii. 24 and Philem. 22 were written from Rome, he is hoping to go to Philippi, and he asks Philemon to have a lodging ready for him at Colossae; so he seems to anticipate that he will be set free. " At my first defence no one stood by me . . . but the Lord stood by me . . . and I was delivered " (2 Tim. iv. 16) might naturally refer to his release. Clement of Rome, in A.D. 96, writing to the Corinthians, says, " Paul reached the boundary of the West," [1] which should mean Spain, and the Muratorian Fragment mentions " the departure of Paul from town on his journey to Spain." Eusebius says he was executed in the Neronian persecution, which did not break out until A.D. 64. We do not know in what year he came to Rome (Acts xxviii), but many scholars believe it was as early as A.D. 59, and two years would bring the date to A.D. 61 ; so there would be an interval of three years for further activity and re-arrest.

On the other hand, we have no other evidence for Paul's release from the imprisonment of Acts xxviii, except the deductions to be drawn from these Pastoral Epistles, and the tradition which asserts he went to Spain ; and that tradition may be itself

---

[1] τὸ τέρμα τῆς δύσεως, 1 Clem. v. 7. But Clement might mean by τέρμα his goal, i.e. Rome. Lake translates " the limits of the West."

nothing but an inference from Rom. xv. 24–28.
" When I have accomplished this " (the collection
for the saints at Jerusalem), " and have sealed to
them this fruit, I will go on by you unto Spain."
Seeing that that was his intention when he wrote
Romans, the tradition may have arisen that he fulfilled it. But it is strange if that is so, and if these
Pastoral Epistles belong to a period after Acts xxviii,
that no mention is made in them of a journey to
Spain. Indeed, because they seem to imply further
activity in the East—Ephesus, Crete, the mainland
of Greece—they rather conflict with the tradition
of any journey to Spain. The inference from these
epistles is that he was released after Acts xxviii, and
went back to the East ; there is also a tradition that
he was released and went west to Spain. The two
are difficult to reconcile, for there is hardly time for
him to have done both before A.D. 64, when he was
said to have been martyred. Therefore some
scholars doubt if he did one or the other, and
think that his imprisonment in Acts xxviii ended
with his death. For (a) Acts is silent as to any
further activity ; and (b) would Luke have left
Paul's speech to the Ephesian elders at Miletus quite
as it is if he had known that Paul was released and
did visit Ephesus again ? " I know that ye all . . .
shall see my face no more." " They all wept sore

. . . sorrowing most of all for the word which he had spoken, that they should behold his face no more." [1]

It is not possible that Paul wrote 1 Timothy and Titus from Rome in his imprisonment in Acts xxviii, —for he is not a prisoner when he writes those letters : and again, if Colossians and Philemon (if not Philippians) were written from Rome in those two years, we cannot make 2 Tim. iv. 10, 11 agree with them. Demas, Crescens, Tychicus, Titus, Mark are all absent from him when he wrote that passage, whereas when he wrote Colossians three of them were present, Tychicus, Mark, and Demas.

Attempts are made to take the passages which make personal allusions in these epistles, and lifting them out of their context to fit them in to Paul's life as we know it up to the end of Acts xxviii. The most thorough investigation of this has been made by P. N. Harrison in *The Problem of the Pastoral Epistles*. He takes five passages and places them as follows :

(1) Titus iii. 12–15. Paul wrote this from Western Macedonia, after he had written the " Severe Letter " to Corinth from Ephesus, which Titus had taken. Paul is waiting in Macedonia for

[1] Acts xx. 25, 38.

Titus—he writes to him at Corinth to join him in Nicopolis (Epirus).

(2) 2 Tim. iv. 13–15, 20, 21a. Paul wrote this from Macedonia, bidding Timothy, who had returned to Ephesus, join him before winter. He had passed through Troas on the way to Macedonia.

(3) 2 Tim. iv. 16–18a. Paul wrote from Caesarea soon after his arrival under escort from Jerusalem. " His first defence " refers then to his speech from the castle steps in Jerusalem, when none of the Christians stood up for him. (Acts xxii. 1 ff.)

(4) 2 Tim. iv. 9–12, 22b. Paul recalls Timothy to Rome. The rest of those who were with Paul when he wrote Colossians have scattered except Luke. The message reached Timothy too late— before he could come Paul had been condemned and wrote his last letter.

(5) 2 Tim. i. 16–18, iii. 10–11, iv. 1, 2, 5, 6–8 are parts of Paul's last letter to Timothy, who is hurrying back to Rome on receipt of the summons in (4).

If Harrison is right, then 2 Timothy is a composite document containing at least four notes of Paul written on different occasions. The inference is that the letter as we have it is not from the hand of Paul.

We have thus to admit that if the personal allusions are to be fitted into Paul's life up to Acts xxviii, then the letters which contain them are in their present form not directly due to the hand of Paul, but come from a disciple writing in his name.

If, on the other hand, Paul was released after Acts xxviii and went to the East, and was later re-arrested, the letters may be genuine : it does not follow that they are.

2. *The Organization of the Church.* These epistles have much to say about the organization of the Church and about the ministry. We know that at the first the organization of the Church was in the hands of the Apostles. They seem to have appointed delegates in the local Churches—presbyters, elders, they are called in Acts xiv. 23 in reference to the Churches of Antioch, Iconium, Lystra, and Derbe. These elders are associated with the Apostles at the Council of Jerusalem in Acts xv. 2, etc. The leaders of the Church at Ephesus are called " elders " and addressed by Paul as bishops.[1] We may presume that the range and function of the " overseership " of the elders were enlarged as the Church grew. In Phil. i. 1 we read of " bishops and deacons." In the Pastoral Epistles it is clear that Timothy and Titus are men with authority, but no official title is given to them. They do not seem to have a permanent position, so they are not

[1] Acts xx. 17–28 ; πρεσβυτέρους 17 ; ἐπισκόπους 28 ; cf. 1 Thess. v. 12.

monarchical bishops such as we find in the second century.

These are the three words in connexion with the ministry : bishop, elder, deacon. The deacon appears to be the lower grade, who, if he serves well, may pass to the higher (1 Tim. iii. 1, 13). But bishop and elder seem two names for one office. The duties assigned to each and the character required in each are identical (cf. 1 Tim. iii. 2–7 and Titus i. 5–9) ; in the latter passage elder and bishop seem interchangeable terms. If so, presbyters would be the title which came from the analogy of the Jewish synagogue, and bishops would be a description of their function as taking oversight. Doubtless, when one individual was required to represent the Church, the title of overseer—bishop—would be applied to him, without implying any difference in status from the other elders.

Some sort of official status of women is implied perhaps in 1 Tim. iii. 11 (cf. Rom. xvi. 1).

There seems to be an order of Church widows (1 Tim. v. 3–16 ; cf. Acts ix. 39, 41). In 1 Timothy the writer seems to be making regulations for an order of widows already in existence.

It is still necessary for a command to be given against women speaking in public (1 Tim. ii. 11–15).

Evidently Paul's instructions in 1 Cor. xiv. 34, 35 are not yet widely known or obeyed.

The ecclesiastical organization does not carry us beyond the conditions in a city such as Ephesus, or a missionary province such as Crete, where Christianity had been well established for a few years, and it would fit any time between about A.D. 60 and 100, that is, it is not inconsistent with authorship by Paul.

3. *Vocabulary and Style.* In vocabulary and style there are some marked divergences from the Pauline letters. Of 897 words, 304 are not found elsewhere in Paul. There are many technical and stereotyped phrases—" Faithful is the saying "—1. i. 15, iii. 1, iv. 9, 2 ii. 11, Titus iii. 8. A Christian hymn is quoted (1 iii. 16). " The faith " often seems to mean " the creed," the doctrines believed (1 iv. 6). " The deposit " (1 vi. 20),[1] " the truth " (1 iii. 15) are similarly used. The stress laid on this is characteristic rather of the man of the second generation than of the pioneer. God is called our Saviour (1 i. 1); elsewhere in Paul Christ is the Saviour.

Instead of the impetuous fervour of Paul the style is correct and diffuse, the syntax is stiffer and more regular.

---

[1] That which is committed unto thee, R.V.

Differences of style and vocabulary, of which these are a few examples, are a strong argument against the authorship of Paul. But of course a man's vocabulary changes with the lapse of years,[1] and it is possible that the amanuensis may have had a larger share in the composition of these than of the earlier letters: but it is hardly likely Paul would have left too much freedom to an amanuensis in giving such important directions as these letters contain.

4. *Doctrine.* In the doctrine there are some important differences between these and the earlier epistles.

Paul believed in the imminence of the Advent. Would he be so much concerned with the organization of the Church as the writer of these epistles is ? It may be answered that Paul was not neglectful at any time of discipline. And the writer of these letters believed in the nearness of the Advent. " I charge thee to keep the commandment, without spot, without reproach, until the appearing of our Lord Jesus Christ " (1 vi. 14). Besides, this writer is not concerned with organization as such, but with the character of those who hold office.

But it is true that he seems to have formularized his beliefs, and to neglect the great Pauline

---

[1] *v.* H. L. Goudge in *A New Commentary on Holy Scripture* (Gore), pp. 579–581.

doctrines of the Fatherhood of God, of the Christian life in Christ, and of the power and witness of the Spirit.

In contrast with the apostolic teaching which is called " the faith," " the truth," " the word of God," " the doctrine that is according to godliness," etc., there were false teachers within the Church. They lay great stress on the importance of their teaching —" desiring to be teachers of the law though they understood neither what they say, nor whereof they confidently affirm " (1 i. 7). They make great efforts to attract followers. " For of these are they that creep into houses, and take captive silly women laden with sins, led away by divers lusts, ever learning and never able to come to the knowledge of the truth " (2 iii. 6 ff). There seem to be two distinct tendencies in them :

1. Jewish—this is specially so in Titus—" For there are many unruly men, vain talkers and deceivers, specially they of the circumcision."[1] " Shun foolish questionings, and genealogies, and strifes, and fightings about the law." [2] So in 1 i. 4–7 : "fables and endless genealogies." Jewish apocryphal legends appeared in great numbers in the first century A.D. The false teachers are clearly not the Judaizers whom Paul attacks in Galatians and Romans.

---

[1] Titus i. 10. [2] Titus iii. 9.

2. The other tendency is Gnostic. This is the reference in 1 iv. 1–5, where the teaching forbidding marriage and commanding to abstain from meats is called " doctrines of devils." These say the " resurrection is past already," [1] that is, that it is only a spiritual resurrection which took place when the Christian was baptized and rose to newness of life. They would have denied the resurrection of the body, because it was part of the Gnostic doctrine that the material was essentially evil. Or they may have said that the true Christian will not die. " The profane babblings and oppositions of the knowledge which is falsely so called " [2] remind us of the Colossian heresy, as does the emphasis on asceticism. [3] There may be a reference to the use of magic in 2 iii. 13: "Evil men and impostors shall wax worse and worse, deceiving and being deceived."

While there are elements here akin to the Gnosticism of the second century, there are none which are quite certainly later than Paul's time. Similar tendencies were found at Corinth and Colossae in his day.

What is of significance is that the writer of these letters does not, after the manner of Paul, meet the false teaching so much with argument as with denunciation.

[1] 2 ii. 18.   [2] 1 vi. 20.   [3] 1 iv. 8

Summary. Each of the four points on which these letters present difficulties can be explained in part at least ; but the question still remains why do they differ so widely from the recognized epistles as to present four problems like these ? Especially the change in the formulation of doctrine and the remarkable divergences in style and language make it not impossible, but improbable, that in their present form they have come from Paul's hand. Most of the personal notes and some other parts may be genuinely his ; but the three letters as we have them have as a whole been built up most likely as general treatises for the guidance of the Church by some devoted disciple of his. If the voice is in parts the authentic voice of Paul, " the hand is that of some Christian teacher in the generation that followed him." There are points of similarity in vocabulary with the Lucan writings.[1] But it is unlikely that Luke had much part in their composition, or they would have been a better literary product. We know that as early as A.D. 140 Marcion rejected them, and P. N. Harrison has

---

[1] There are several words in these epistles, e.g. ἁμαρτωλός, ἐπισκοπή, ὅσιος κ.τ.λ., which occur more frequently in Luke-Acts than in the Pauline Epistles. One or both of the quotations in Paul's speech at Athens (Acts xvii. 28) may be from Epimenides, the Cretan poet, whose description of the Cretans is quoted in Tit. i. 12. *v.* Lake, *The Beginnings of Christianity*, vol. v, pp. 246–251. Luke was alone with Paul at the time of his approaching death (2 Tim. iv. 11).

shown that in vocabulary they are closer akin to the Apostolic Fathers than to the Pauline Epistles. But they may have been known to Clement of Rome in A.D. 96, and they are well attested in the latter half of the second century. But we may conclude with Dr. Lock : " If they were not written as they stand by St. Paul, they probably incorporate some earlier notes of his ; the whole was written by one who thought himself a devoted follower of St. Paul, whose mind was steeped in the very language of St. Paul's letters : and this attempt was accepted by the Church as true to its memory of what St. Paul had been and taught." [1] If they are later than Paul, the probable order of writing was 2 Timothy, Titus, 1 Timothy, because the greater number of the personal allusions in 2 Timothy point to its being nearer the lifetime of Paul ; and the greater severity in the treatment of the false teachers in Titus and 1 Timothy, and the possible literary dependence of these two letters on 1 Peter are regarded as arguments for their later date. But the three cannot be later than A.D. 110 and are more likely to have been written near the end of the first century.

Pseudonymity. All the books that belonged to the popular apocalyptic literature were pseudonymous.

[1] *Commentary on the Pastoral Epistles,* International Critical Commentary, p. xxxi.

Historians had been accustomed to embellish their works with speeches which they themselves composed and attributed to historical characters. So there was a legitimate method which produced books in all good faith under the name of some revered teacher. " This was done with the honest and humble aim of edifying the faithful. The disciple would conceal his own name as he sought to reproduce what he believed would have been the ideas and instructions of an honoured master. There was no literary ambition in the practice, but rather the consciousness that through the pages of the disciple the apostle still spoke " (Moffatt).[1]

[1] " The Formation of the N.T.," in the *Abingdon Bible Commentary,* p. 855.

PART III
THE EPISTLE TO THE HEBREWS

CHAPTER XII

THE EPISTLE TO THE HEBREWS

This is put among the letters in the New Testament. But it lacks some of the familiar marks of a letter : the writer's name and greeting, and the name of the readers at the beginning ; the name of the amanuensis and bearer of the letter, and the sign that the writer has taken the pen and signed it—at the end. The style suggests an oration rather than a letter : the author calls it " a word of exhortation."[1]

The MSS. have the title πρὸς Ἑβραίους (to the Hebrews). No other title was known, unless it is referred to as " a forged letter of Paul to the Alexandrians "[2] in the Muratorian Fragment. The vagueness of the title—unlike the letters of Paul—has led to emendations[3]—πρὸς βερναίους or βεροιαίους (to the Beroeans), whose interest in the Scriptures is noted in Acts xvii. 11 ; or πρὸς ἑταιρούς (to his friends). But these are mere guesses.

The word " Hebrew " does not occur in the letter itself. If it is the correct title, it might be

---

[1] xiii. 22.
[2] Fertur etiam ad Laudecenses, alia ad Alexandrinos Pauli nomine finctae ad haeresem Marcionis.
[3] Klostermann.

meant in a symbolic sense, but it is natural to understand it of those who were of Jewish race, but not necessarily living in Palestine.

Destination. The characteristics of the society addressed can be briefly described thus :

1. It was a society, not Hebrew Christians generally, for the writer hopes to visit them (xiii. 23). He speaks of them as brethren (xiii. 22) and beloved (vi. 9), but not as children. He is not the founder of the Church, if they are a Church, but their friend rather than their spiritual father.

2. The society was not mixed—Jews and Gentiles—for there is no hint of anything like the Judaistic controversy.

3. A small body seems addressed and separate from its leaders. He blames them because they were in an elementary stage when they ought to have been teachers [1] : this would hardly apply to all the members of a Christian ecclesia. He bids them salute all in authority over them and all the saints,[2] as if his readers are a small group within a large society.

4. They had not been eye-witnesses, nor had the writer of this letter, for he speaks of " (salvation) which having at the first been spoken through the Lord, was confirmed unto us by them that heard." [3]

[1] v. 12.   [2] xiii. 24.   [3] ii. 3.

They were of the second generation of Christians ; but they had been evangelized by those who had heard the Lord.

5. They had endured some persecution, but not unto blood (xii. 4).

These facts do not settle the question whether the readers were Jews or Gentiles.   The reasons, apart from the title, for believing that the readers were Jewish Christians are :

1. The writer eloquently expounds Christianity as the perfection of Judaism.   If his readers were in danger of relapsing into heathenism, he would not have stressed this so much.   But the emphasis he lays upon it suggests they were in danger of drifting back to Judaism.

2. Would he have used the Old Testament, as he has, unless it still had authority for them, even if they forsook Christianity ?

3. "Let us go forth unto him without the camp"[1] seems an exhortation to his readers to cut themselves free from Judaism.

On the other hand, J. Moffatt and E. F. Scott maintain that the letter was meant for Gentiles, and that the title is a mistake, for these reasons :

1. The writer always quotes from the Old Testament according to the Septuagint, not according to

[1] xiii. 13.

the Hebrew. And the appeal to the Old Testament was as valid for Gentile Christians as for Jews, and formed the natural basis for an attempt to present Christianity as the religion of the New Covenant.

In answer to this it might be argued that the Jews accepted the Old Testament because they were Jews; that the Gentile Christians accepted it because they were Christians. If the readers were in danger of drifting from Christianity, the Old Testament would have had no authority any longer for them, if they were Gentiles—only if they were Jews.

2. Moffatt, however, further claims that there is no proof that they were in danger of relapsing into Judaism. The writer says nothing about Jewish ordinances as a rule of life.

3. There is no mention of the Temple and Circumcision. This is strange if he is writing to Jews.

The destination of the letter is thus a difficult problem. If it was addressed to Jews, who were tempted to forsake Christianity for Judaism, it can hardly have been written to Jerusalem, or to any Christian society in Palestine. For the writer implies that his readers had not been hearers of the Lord,[1] and had not propagated the faith.[2] More-

[1] ii. 3.　　　　[2] v. 12.

over, Greek is the original language, and the Septuagint is their Bible. Antioch, because of the supposition that Barnabas was the author, Caesarea, on the ground that Luke may have written it, have little to support them. Alexandria has a stronger claim because of the philosophic character of the theme, and would be supported if it could be shown that Apollos was the author. Ephesus has been suggested for the same two reasons—the Alexandrianism (the Fourth Gospel is Alexandrian, and that is associated with Ephesus), and the authorship of Apollos, who is associated with Ephesus in Acts.[1] "They of Italy salute you"[2] suggests the readers lived in Italy, and some of their compatriots join in the writer's greeting. If so, Rome may have some claim to be the destination of the letter. Nairne imagines the letter was written to a little clan, a household community, part of a larger Church: the writer's exhortations not to forsake the assembling of themselves together,[3] and to "obey them that have the rule over you,"[4] suggest they were never quite at home in the community of Christians to which they belonged. Perhaps the environment was rude for these intellectuals, to whom the philosophic argument of this letter is directed. Perhaps there was a strong appeal to

[1] xviii. 24 ff.   [2] xiii. 24.   [3] x. 25.   [4] xiii. 17.

them as patriotic Jews to throw in their lot with their countrymen in Palestine in the crisis of A.D. 65–66, which led to the destruction of Jerusalem. They were disturbed when they saw so much that they held sacred in imminent danger of disaster: the writer assures them that the hour has come when they must break with traditional Judaism. " Go forth unto him without the camp." [1]   " He taketh away the first, that he may establish the second." [2] They will see " the removing of those things that are shaken, as of things that have been made, that those things which are not shaken may remain." [3]

If the letter was written to Gentile Christians, the destination of a house-church in Rome, or somewhere in Italy, is as likely as any other from xiii. 24, but the association with the critical situation in Palestine would not be true.

F. D. V. Narborough [4] has suggested that the readers were Gentile Christians in danger of being led astray by false teaching such as led Paul to write to the Colossians ; and if so, they may have lived in and near Ephesus. The Colossian heresy taught the worship of angels, asceticism, observance of sabbaths, and meats, etc., and seems to have been based on the Gnostic dualism of spirit and matter

---

[1] xiii. 13.   [2] x. 9.   [3] xii. 27.
[4] In his commentary in the *Clarendon Bible*, p. 20 ff.

—good and evil. The writer of this letter emphasizes the superiority of Jesus to Moses,[1] the giver of the Law, and to angels through whom it was spoken.[2] He warns his readers : "Be not carried away by divers and strange teachings : for it is good that the heart be stablished by grace ; not by meats, wherein they that occupied themselves were not profited."[3] Would he have called Judaism "divers and strange teachings" if the readers were in danger of drifting back to that ? But the part which the sacrificial system plays in the argument of Hebrews seems hardly consistent with a refutation of incipient Gnosticism such as was rife at Colossae.

On the whole an argument which proves the superiority of Christianity to Judaism and its finality as *the* religion, and which sets forth Jesus as the great High Priest, supported by abundant quotations from the Septuagint, would seem most appropriately addressed to some small circle of cultured Jewish Christians. When read in the light of such notes as the letter contains about the circumstances of the readers, Nairne's suggestion of Rome as the destination of the letter has perhaps more to commend it than any other.

Date. The date of the letter cannot be certainly

---

[1] iii. 2–6.   [2] ii. 5–10.   [3] xiii. 9.

determined. But a generation of Christians had already passed away.[1] There had been time enough for religious growth[2] and for changes in religious feeling.[3] There is no clear reference to the destruction of Jerusalem. The controversy about the Law is over. It cannot be later than about A.D. 85, for Clement of Rome used it. Therefore somewhere between about A.D. 60 and 85 seems reasonable. Nairne dates it about A.D. 65–66, when the siege had begun. Those who think it was sent to a group of Gentile Christians date it A.D. 80–85. If it relates to a danger like that of the Colossian heresy, about A.D. 70 is the date suggested.

Author. In the Eastern Church the Epistle was received as scripture from early times, but in the West, because of the doubts about its authorship, it had no secure place until the fourth century, and then it won its place because it was attributed to Paul. It was natural to associate an epistle against Judaism with Paul. Clement of Alexandria, according to Eusebius, said Paul wrote it in the Hebrew language and Luke translated it into Greek. But the use of the Septuagint for Old Testament quotation shows that that is unwarranted. Modern scholars are sure of only one thing about the author-

---

[1] ii. 3, xiii. 7.   [2] v. 11, 12.   [3] x. 32.

ship, that whoever wrote it, it was not Paul. The style and vocabulary, the attitude to the Law, the conception of Faith, and the High Priesthood of our Lord are not Pauline. Moreover, the author claims that he and his readers have received their knowledge of the gospel from those who heard the Lord.[1] Paul is most emphatic that he received his gospel from no man.[2]

Tertullian attributes the epistle to Barnabas—the only member of the Pauline circle who would have sufficient authority to send such a letter. The writer calls his letter "the word of exhortation."[3] Barnabas is interpreted in Acts iv. 36 as one able to give exhortation (υἱὸς παρακλήσεως). But we have no evidence to connect Barnabas with Rome, or with Alexandrian thought. The Epistle of Barnabas (so-called) is similarly based on the Old Testament and on Alexandrian thought, but the attitude of the writer to the Levitical ritual and to the Temple makes common authorship impossible. The reference to Timothy suggests that the author was a junior, not a senior, member of the Pauline circle.[4]

Among other suggestions are : Luke, because of certain coincidences between the style of the Lucan writings and Hebrews. But the literary relation-

---

[1] ii. 3.   [2] Gal. i. 1, 12.   [3] xiii. 22.   [4] xiii. 23.

ship is not strong enough to warrant such a conclusion.

Clement of Rome—a man of mental calibre much inferior to the author of Hebrews.

Silas : because there are striking coincidences between 1 Peter and Hebrews, it is suggested that Silas might have been the amanuensis of the one, and the author of the other. But neither Clement nor Silas is associated with Hebrews by tradition ; and we should expect Silas to show more traces of Paul's than of Peter's influence.

Luther was the first to suggest Apollos—the Alexandrian Jew—" mighty in the scriptures " (Acts xviii. 24). Apollos was eloquent—the author of this book was an orator. The reference to baptisms in vi. 2 might have special significance for Apollos, who knew John's baptism before he was converted by Priscilla and Aquila. If Apollos be the author, it would explain the traces of Pauline thought and yet the independence of the epistle.

But was the word confirmed unto Apollos by those who heard the Lord ?[1] Was it not by Priscilla and Aquila ? Would not Clement of Rome have mentioned Apollos when he quotes this letter, and when he alludes to the " Apollos party " at Corinth ? But, on the other hand, if the writer is

[1] ii. 3.

warning the readers against such false teaching as had disturbed the Church at Colossae, and if they lived in or around Ephesus, that would be an additional reason for connecting Apollos with it.

Harnack suggested Priscilla and Aquila wrote the epistle to the Church which met in their house in Rome.[1]   Harnack notes that : (1) the author's name was lost ; how could that happen if it was written by any of those already mentioned ?   Was it intentionally suppressed ?   (2) The author represents not only himself, but one or more jointly responsible with him.[2]   Aquila is hardly important enough—his wife seems to have been more so : she was no ordinary woman who could instruct Apollos (Acts xviii. 26).   But why was the name lost ?   This is the most significant part of the argument.   About no other name can an explanation be given why it was lost.   But if the writer was a woman, there would be a strong temptation to suppress the name. Paul disliked women teachers.   Clement of Rome would not have mentioned the authoress of the epistle he is quoting, when he is reminding the Corinthians of the letters which Paul wrote to

[1] Rom. xvi. 5.
[2] xiii. 18–19, I and we.   (But this may be nothing more than the common alternation of I or we in letters, cf. 2 Macc. ii. 29, and the papyri letters.)

them. Women teachers soon fell into disrepute in the early Church.

Priscilla and Aquila were cultured Hellenistic Jews who may well have been conversant with Alexandrian thought. All the arguments for Apollos may be used with almost equal force for the teacher of Apollos. Even Ephesus as a destination is quite as possible with Priscilla as authoress as with Apollos.

The alteration of the feminine to the masculine participle (διηγούμενον)[1] would naturally have been made in very early copies, when Priscilla's name was no longer associated with the epistle. Possibly there was a formal opening of the letter in her name, and it was deliberately suppressed.

In support of Priscilla, it is pointed out that the author has the attitude and outlook of a pilgrim, the patriarchs were strangers and pilgrims on the earth—they desire a heavenly country.[2] There are many references to nautical terms.[3] The argument has to do with the Tabernacle—the sacred tent—Priscilla and Aquila were tent-makers.

It is consistent with the theory that the writer may have been a woman that there is shown special interest in parenthood and childhood [4]: in the

---

[1] xi. 32.   [2] xi. 13–16.
[3] iii. 6, 14 (κατέχω); vi. 19, the anchor of the soul; xiii. 9 (παραφέρομαι).
[4] v. 12.

references to Melchizedek[1] ; to Sarah[2] ; to Moses—
" a goodly child "[3] ; to the discipline of sons.[4]

Dibelius [5] and others maintain that the epistle is a
treatise, the letter form is a literary illusion, and it is
therefore idle to attempt to identify the author or
the readers.   But there are personal notes which
do not seem due to literary art but to personal relationship between the writer and the readers.
Attempts to separate ch. xiii. from this epistle and
attribute it to Paul as part of one of his letters
have little or nothing to commend them.

Theme and Message.   The theme is the finality of
the revelation in Jesus the Son of God.   God had
never left Himself without witness, but in the last
days He has revealed Himself in One Who is Son.
The Son is superior to angels, not in spite of but
because of His incarnation and death.[6]   He is
greater than Moses, a servant in the house.[7]   Since
it was the purpose of His coming to bring many
sons to glory, it was fitting that He should be in all
things like unto His brethren.[8]   (To this the writer
returns again and again.)   Christ shared in the
divine nature, but had a complete understanding
of and sympathy with humanity.   He alone knows

---

[1] vii. 3.   [2] xi. 11.   [3] xi. 23.   [4] xii. 7.
[5] *Geschichte der urchristlichen Literatur*, vol. ii. s. 49.
[6] ii. 9–10.   [7] iii. 5–6.   [8] ii. 17, 18

the full power of temptation, for He alone has resisted it to the end. He is thus the perfect representative of humanity in the sight of God. He is therefore the ideal High Priest. He needed no offering for Himself (unlike the Jewish high priest) : He brought the complete dedication of Himself to the will of God.[1] When He had offered one sacrifice for sins for ever, He sat down on the right hand of God.[2] His work was done for ever. For what He did was not done in the tabernacle made with hands. His ministry was in the ideal Tabernacle, and inaugurated the new, that is, the ideal, covenant foreshadowed by Jeremiah.[3] Therefore He secured for men what the Jewish sacrifices could never secure : He dedicated a new and living way [4] into the divine presence : He won forgiveness of sins and fellowship of man with God.

The writer interprets the Old Testament with a freedom which his Alexandrian training had made familiar to him. The old covenant was the shadow, not the substance, the symbol, not the reality. The tabernacle Moses built was a pattern of the heavenly, the sacrifices of the priests were a prophecy of the sacrifice of the eternal High Priest, Jesus. And in the mystic figure of Melchizedek he finds such a priesthood as that of Jesus foreshadowed. Like

[1] x. 5-10.   [2] x. 12.   [3] viii. 8.   [4] x. 20.

Melchizedek, Jesus was both priest and king, and though He appeared in the temporal order, He had an eternal significance.   What He had done in time was valid for all time—the redemption He won was " eternal redemption." [1]

But the author sees more in the Old Testament than these allegorical methods of exegesis suppose. The Old Testament is the record of those who, while living in the world of physical senses, were aware of the eternal world ; of men and women who were convinced of the reality of this unseen world, sure that God had spoken and could be trusted to keep His word.   Faith for Paul meant personal trust in Christ.   Faith for this writer is defined and illustrated in the long and eloquent eleventh chapter—it is loyalty to spiritual values which are not seen by the sense, but which are behind and beyond all the chances and changes of human life.   He unveils a portrait gallery of the saints and heroes of the past, of whom " the world was not worthy," and shows that this was the thing that characterized them, and inspired them to be pilgrims desiring a better country—" a city which hath the foundations, whose builder and maker is God."   Because of Jesus the assurance of faith is more real than it had ever been.   In Him has been

[1] ix. 12.

T.—6*

given the realization of the promises to the fathers. Faith sees Him seated at the right hand of God, faith clings to Him as the divine reality, " the very truth of things, all that is meant by God." This is his philosophy of history—let his readers recall the noble endeavours and costly sacrifices of the men of old, that they may be more conscious of the opportunities of the present, more eager to live worthily of the heritage which is theirs, more tenacious of their hope for the future.[1]

Canonicity. The epistle was known to Clement of Rome, rejected by Marcion, and is not mentioned in the Muratorian Fragment. The African Church, except Tertullian, does not seem to have known it. In Alexandria it was accepted as canonical from the earliest time that we hear of it, but in the West it was not recognized until the fourth century, and then it was received because it was assumed that it had been written by Paul, and through the influence of Jerome and Augustine.

[1] xii. 1-2.

PART IV

THE CATHOLIC EPISTLES

CHAPTER XIII

THE CATHOLIC EPISTLES: THE EPISTLE OF JAMES

Clement of Alexandria calls the letter about the Apostolic Decrees in Acts xv the "Catholic Epistle of all the Apostles." Origen describes the Epistle of Barnabas and the Epistles of John, Peter, and Jude, as Catholic. Eusebius says that James is the first of the so-called Catholic Epistles.[1]

THE EPISTLE OF JAMES

Canonicity. The Epistle of James was known to the author of the *Shepherd* of Hermas and perhaps to Clement of Rome. So the epistle may be said to have been known in the Church in Rome about the end of the first century and the beginning of the second. After that we have no trace of it in the other Apostolic Fathers; nor is it mentioned in the Muratorian Fragment. The earliest reference to it under the name of James is by Origen, and

---

[1] A secondary and later meaning was derived from the use of the word in reference to the Church. An epistle was " catholic " in spirit and accepted by the " catholic," i.e. universal Church. So " catholic " is applied to a book to mean canonical.

v. Jülicher-Fascher, *Einleitung in das Neue Testament*, s. 186–189.

he does not seem to regard it as Scripture.[1]
Eusebius says some regard it as spurious, but he
quotes it as Scripture. It was not until the fourth
century that it was accepted into the Canon of the
Western Church, and only in the fifth century did it
find a place in the Canon of the Churches of Syria.

Authorship. The writer calls himself " James,
a servant of God and of the Lord Jesus Christ."

The early Christian references suppose this is
James, the brother of the Lord,[2] and the first bishop
of Jerusalem.[3] J. B. Mayor finds support for this
in the tone of authority which the writer assumes;
in the similarity between the language of this
epistle and the speech of James at the Council of
Jerusalem in Acts xv; in the Jewish tone (James,
according to tradition, was one who loved and kept
the Law); in the fact that there seem to be many
reminiscences, though not actual quotations, of the
Sermon on the Mount. Mayor thinks that he does
not call himself the brother of the Lord because of
our Lord's words, " whosoever shall do the will of
God, the same is my brother, and sister, and mother "
(Mark iii. 35).

But the doubt about the epistle's canonicity is

---

[1] *Comm. in Joan.* xix. 6 : ὡς ἐν τῇ φερομένῃ Ἰακώβου Ἐπιστολῇ ἀνέγνωμεν.
[2] Mark vi. 3.
[3] Gal. i. 18, 19, ii. 1-10 ; Acts xv. 13, etc.

difficult to explain, if James, the Lord's brother, is the author ; and while we have evidence that the epistle was known at the end of the first century, or shortly after, we have no hint of its connexion with James until Origen's time. Moffatt and others therefore deny the traditional authorship, adducing as additional evidence against it : (1) The controversy about the Law and the admission of the Gentiles is over—was this so by the year A.D. 62 when we know James was martyred? (2) The epistle presupposes a knowledge of the Pauline Epistles, and that makes it later in the century. (3) Could James write such good Greek ? it is asked. The style of the Greek and the Greek ideas and illustrations[1] show the writer's acquaintance with Hellenistic culture and literature. (4) The absence of any reference to the resurrection and the Messianic claims of Jesus. This is the more remarkable since the resurrection played an important part in James's conversion.[2]

Moffatt suggests, in the light of these facts, that the author was a teacher of the Church called James, of whom we know nothing else.

Ropes and other scholars think the epistle was

---

[1] E.g. iii. 2 ff.

[2] According to Jerome, who is quoting from the " Gospel according to the Hebrews " ; v. M. R. James, *The Apocryphal New Testament*, pp. 3, 4.

pseudonymous : it was written under the name of
James, the Lord's brother, and so survived in
Palestine, but was forgotten elsewhere, until perhaps Origen brought it to Alexandria, and it
gradually won a place in the Canon.

Other theories are more drastic—Spitta[1] suggested it was an adaptation of pre-Christian Jewish
work, because there is nothing definitely Christian
in it, except i. 1, ii. 1, " our Lord Jesus Christ,"
and he suggests the name has been interpolated
there. But phrases such as " the word of truth,"
" the honourable name," and " the coming of the
Lord," show that the lack of Christian material has
been exaggerated.

J. H. Moulton[2] suggested that James wrote this
epistle to the unconverted Jews. He did not mention the name of Jesus, but introduced many of the
sayings of Jesus into his epistle to win his countrymen by the intrinsic merit of these sayings. He
wished to shame them out of their unbelief based
on party spirit (iii. 14, 16). The success of the
appeal was ruined by his martyrdom as a Christian.
The Jews ceased to have any regard for him, because he had been martyred as a Christian ; and the
Christians ignored his book because it was written

---

[1] *v.* Jülicher-Fascher, *Einleitung in das Neue Testament*, s. 210–213.
[2] *Expositor*, July 1907.

for Jews and had so little distinctively Christian teaching. It was, however, treasured in a narrow circle, and at last came to have its place in the Canon because of its association with the great name of James.

It is difficult, however, to believe that James would have suppressed so much that was distinctively Christian, e.g. the Messianic claim of Jesus, in order to commend Christianity to his own countrymen. Neither Peter nor Paul adopted such methods ; would James ?

F. C. Burkitt [1] has suggested that James, the Lord's brother, wrote in Aramaic to some Jewish Christian community very likely in Jerusalem. This was freely translated into Greek (hence the style of the Greek), perhaps by Hegesippus, who found it in the Greek-speaking Gentile Christian Church of Aelia Capitolina, when it was beginning to adopt James as its ecclesiastical ancestor. Hegesippus turned it into a general epistle to the twelve tribes of the Dispersion—i.e. to Gentile Christians, the new Israel.

B. H. Streeter [2] thinks that the epistle was written in Rome in the latter part of the century, because in Rome we find the first trace of it. The Roman

[1] *Christian Beginnings*, pp. 65 ff.
[2] *The Primitive Church*, pp. 189 ff.

Church knew the name of the author, and did not ascribe it to an Apostle, or it would at once have found its place in the Canon. In the second century an Alexandrian scholar prefixed the name of James, because he was the one in apostolic times whose thought was farthest removed from that of Paul. This gave it a new lease of life, and won it the support of the Church in Aelia Capitolina, and eventually secured its admission to the Canon.

Neither Moulton's nor Burkitt's attempts to defend the traditional authorship are sufficient to meet the many difficulties in the way. The epistle was either by an unknown James, or pseudonymous; written by someone who felt that he was the interpreter of the James who stood in such high regard in Jerusalem, both among Jews as well as Christians, in the middle of the first century.

Date. If James, the Lord's brother, was the author, then the epistle must have been written before A.D. 62, when he was martyred.[1] Mayor puts it as early as A.D. 40, and thinks Paul is answering it in Romans in the "faith and works" passages. If that is so, then it is the earliest book in the New Testament.

---

[1] Josephus, *Ant. Jud.* XX. ix. 1. Hegesippus ap. Eus., *Hist. Eccles.*, ii. 23. Probably the account in Josephus is the more accurate.

If this traditional authorship is denied, it must be placed before A.D. 90, if Clement of Rome and the *Shepherd* of Hermas knew it. It is hardly possible to be more definite than between A.D. 70 and 90—after the controversy about the Law was ended.

But if it was originally written in the first, the epistolary form may have been imposed upon it in the second century. The lack of apostolicity and its apparent contradiction of Paul's teaching about the relative merits of faith and works may have prevented its winning recognition until a later period. There is nothing in the epistle which suggests it was written to Jewish Christians in very early days ; it seems a homily addressed to Christians generally, " exposed to the ordinary trials and temptations which met the later stages of the apostolic age " (Moffatt).

Leading Ideas. Ropes describes the epistle as an imitation of the diatribe. The epistle has the terse gnomic style of the Wisdom literature : parallels to the books of Proverbs, Wisdom, and Ecclesiasticus[1] are many. To the author wisdom is what faith is to Paul, hope to Peter, love to John—the essence of

[1] E.g. Jas. i. 5, Prov. ii. 6 ; Jas. iv. 13, 14, Prov. xxvii. 1 ; Jas. i. 12, Wis. v. 16 ; Jas. iv. 14, Wis. ii. 4 ; Jas. i. 19, Ecclus. iv. 29, v. 11 ; Jas. ii. 1–6, Ecclus. x. 19–24.

the Christian life. There are passages (iv. 1–10 and
v. 1–6) which are inspired by the same spirit as is
felt in Amos v. 11–15, 21–24, Isa. i. 2–17.

Much of the epistle is grouped round three or
four main ideas : trial or temptation (i. 2–16) ; the
hearing and the doing of the word (i. 19–27) ; the
relation of rich and poor (ii. 1–13) ; things that
deny and destroy the brotherhood in the Christian
community as " respect of persons " (ii. 1) ; and an
unbridled tongue (iii. 5). Streeter thinks that the
reference to the man with a gold ring and fine
clothing coming into your synagogue[1] is specially
appropriate in Rome. For there the word " synagogue " was used of the place where Christians
meet for worship. (It is so used by Hermas three
times.) And we know that some of the Roman
aristocracy did attach themselves to the Christian
faith at the end of the century. Against world-
liness and factiousness the author holds up the ideal
of a life inspired by " the wisdom that is from
above," which is " first pure, then peaceable,
gentle, easy to be intreated, full of mercy and
good fruits, without variance, without hypocrisy "
(iii. 17).

Faith and Works. The passage that has roused
most debate is ii. 14–26. It was this which caused

[1] ii. 2.

Martin Luther to call James "eine stroherne Epistel."
Comparing this with Rom. iii. 28 and iv. 1–6, we
find James and Paul quoting Gen. xv. 6, " Abraham
believed God, and it was reckoned unto him for
righteousness," but apparently drawing contra-
dictory conclusions out of it. The debate has been
upon the question, Was James replying to Paul or
Paul to James? Mayor maintained James was the
more elementary, and Paul was turning aside his
argument, and stating in more guarded language
what they both held in common. It seems much
more likely that James is protesting against misunderstanding, it may be even deliberate misrepresentation, of Paul's teaching. "A man is
justified by faith apart from the works of the law "[1]
is a discovery made by Paul which had worked a
revolution within him. It may well be that James
had never read Romans; but whether he had or not,
he knew that if faith was a profession of belief, and
no more, if there was no moral character or conduct
which corresponded to his belief, that faith cannot save a man.[2] James means by faith assent
to the doctrines of Christianity. But he insists that
mere belief, e.g. in God, devoid of any works, sig-
nifies that a man is on no higher level than the
daemons : they have faith and they show it in their

[1] Rom. iii. 28.   [2] ii. 14.

terror (ii. 19). He quotes two examples : Abraham, who was justified by his offering of Isaac ; i.e. his faith co-operated with his works (Paul had quoted Abraham as the great example of faith without works). Rahab is the other example who was justified by her works : " She received the messengers, and sent them out another way " (ii. 25). Perhaps Rahab was quoted by the antinomians, whom James denounces.

It is possible that justification by faith or works was debated in the Rabbinic schools.[1] But whether this was so or not, the antithesis between faith and works, as Paul states it, is original to him, and is not found in Jewish thought. But Paul means by faith personal trust and surrender, in which man throws himself on God. He would not have called the belief of the daemons faith. Paul was fully alive to the danger in misrepresenting his teaching. " What shall we say then ? Shall we continue in sin, that grace may abound ? God forbid " (Rom. vi. 1). " Shall we sin, because we are not under law but under grace ? God forbid " (Rom. vi. 15). If Paul had read James, he would not have objected, though it was not his way of putting it. If James had read Romans, he would have seen that his words were quite inadequate to meet its arguments. For

[1] v. R. J. Knowling, *The Epistle of St. James*, pp. xlii ff.

James " conduct is three-fourths of life," as Matthew Arnold put it ; but neither James nor Paul would have agreed that the other part does not matter. Both would have insisted that the first thing to do with faith is to live by it.

CHAPTER XIV

THE FIRST EPISTLE OF PETER

Canonicity. This epistle, with the exception of
1 John, is the only Catholic epistle which was widely
known and accepted as authoritative in the early
Church. It is referred to in 2 Pet. iii. 1. There is
some evidence for believing that Clement of Rome
knew it. Eusebius says it was used by Papias. The
first clear reference is in Polycarp, but he does not
quote it by name. The Muratorian Fragment does
not mention it—but Zahn has cleverly amended a
line to include it.[1] Irenaeus, Tertullian, Clement of
Alexandria, and Origen, all quote by name, and
there is no doubt about it afterwards.

Authorship. Many modern scholars deny the
Apostolic authorship for the following reasons : (1)
while Polycarp quotes it, he does not mention Peter's
name in his quotation, though he names Paul twice.
Irenaeus is the first to name Peter as the author. (2)
The style shows a command of Greek and a knowledge of the Septuagint, which we should hardly
expect from a Galilean fisherman. (But if Silas

---

[1] As restored in Greek, Πέτρου [ἐπιστολὴ μία, ἥν] μόνην ἀποδεχόμεθα.
In the Latin it refers to an Apocalypse of Peter.

was his amanuensis, he may have had a considerable share in the composition.) (3) The affinity in thought and language with the Pauline Epistles is such that it has even been claimed that the writer was more influenced by Paul than by Jesus. (But this is an exaggeration [1]; besides, the writer and his amanuensis might have been influenced by Paul without having read either Romans or Ephesians or any other of his letters.)

Most of those who have questioned the Petrine authorship have associated the epistle with Rome. But Streeter,[2] while mentioning the points already stated, emphasizes further difficulties.

(4) We should not have expected Peter to call himself " a fellow-elder," [3] for apostle and elder were not the same; (5) nor could Peter be accurately described as " a witness of the sufferings of Christ " [3] : he was not present at the crucifixion. (6) " The epistle arose at a time when Christianity was a crime punishable by death." [4] That would be during Nero's reign, after Paul's death. Would Peter, writing from Rome in that hour, have impressed upon his readers the duty of obedience to the imperial government,[5] as a government which was sent by God " for vengeance on evil-doers and

---

[1] v. C. H. Dodd, The Apostolic Preaching, pp. 97-100.
[2] The Primitive Church, pp. 115 ff.   [3] v. 1.
[4] iv. 15-16.   [5] ii. 13-17.

praise to those that do well "? And would he
have called Rome " Babylon " ?[1] Streeter is re-
luctantly led to the conclusion that the epistle is
not by the Apostle, and does not emanate from
Rome. The epistolary form has been impressed
upon an older document by a later editor. The
original is a combination of : (a) a sermon (i. 3–
iv. 11) to a group of newly baptized persons, and
(b) a pastoral letter (iv. 12–v. 11), in reference to a
fiery trial of an unexpected character. This sermon
and letter were, Streeter guesses, by Aristion, the
first bishop of Smyrna—one of the two " who were
reckoned to rank after the Apostles as authorities
for the authentic teaching of Christ and were styled
Disciples of the Lord—the other was John the
Elder." [2]

The pastoral letter was addressed by the bishop
to meet the same situation as is referred to in
Apoc. ii. 10—the message to Smyrna. Streeter
continues the story in postulating that these two,
the sermon and the letter, were cherished at Smyrna
and were written on one papyrus roll. Later the
address and salutation were added, perhaps in Sinope,
in Pliny's time, A.D. 112, when he had begun to
persecute Christians, to give counsel to those who
needed it under the authority of an apostolic name.

1 V. 13.   2 Eus. (quoting Papias), *Hist. Eccles.* iii. 39.

Brilliant as these conjectures are, they invite us to take many leaps in the dark.

Is it so clear that the persecution mentioned implies a date outside Peter's life ? Who would have thought of inventing Silas as amanuensis to Peter ? Can we build so much upon the silence of Polycarp about Peter ? If Peter was already associated by tradition with the gospel of Mark, there was the less reason for associating his name with this epistle, and especially for making him the author of a letter to provinces in which Paul had been the pioneer missionary.

It is certainly likely that this epistle would never have been included in the Canon but for Peter's name being inscribed in it ; but there are elements in the tone of the epistle, and in the circumstances of the readers, which make it not impossible to accept the traditional authorship.

The dominant notes are hope,[1] self-control,[2] obedience,[3] humility,[4] endurance of persecution.[5]

These notes are not proof in any sense that the author was he who had undergone such experiences as changed the impulsive and unstable disciple of the Gospels into a pillar of the Church in Acts—

[1] i. 3.   [2] i. 13.   [3] ii. 13.
[4] iii. 8.   [5] iv. 13, 14.

but they are consistent with what we should expect
from Peter. We cannot attach much importance
to the similarity of Peter's speeches in Acts
with this epistle or the affinities between it and
Hebrews. There was a heritage of religious
ideas which belonged to the early Christian
Church and in which all the writers of the first
century share.

We might expect that Peter would dwell more
upon the details of our Lord's life, if we did not
remember that these played but a small part in the
apostolic preaching (κήρυγμα). There are references which are consistent with the writer as an eye-
witness, though of course they might be due to
knowledge of the Gospels and could then have
been written by anyone in the second century :
" girding up the loins of your mind " (i. 13) ;
" gird yourselves with humility " (v. 5 : cp. Luke
xii. 35, Jn. xiii. 4, 14) ; " Whom not having seen ye
love " (i. 8 : *ye* not *we*) ; " Who, when he was
reviled, reviled not again ; when he suffered,
threatened not " (ii. 25) ; " I, who am a fellow-
elder and a witness of the sufferings of Christ "
(v. 1). It is true Peter was not a witness of the
trial and crucifixion, and in his speeches in Acts,
Peter, as Streeter says, " goes out of his way to
call himself a ' witness ' of *the Resurrection*, which he

truly was." But when writing to encourage those who were undergoing " the fiery trial," [1] Peter may well have claimed an intimate knowledge of the sufferings of the Lord.[2]

Circumstances of the Readers and Date. The readers are described as " sojourners of the Dispersion in (the provinces of) Pontus, Galatia, Cappadocia, Asia, and Bithynia." No very satisfactory theory of the order of those provinces has been put forward. But we may interpret the terms " sojourners " and " Dispersion " in a symbolic sense, as describing the condition of Christians—the true Israel—scattered in an alien world, where they have no abiding city—exiled from their heavenly home until the " Shepherd and Bishop of their souls " shall appear.[3] They may have been both Jews and Gentiles—more especially the latter.

The nature of the persecution in view is not quite clear. Was it organized by the State ? It has been maintained that the situation portrayed is before the Neronian persecution has broken out : there are no references to martyrdom for the Gospel, nor to imprisonment, as though Christianity were illegal. The readers are called to endure " manifold temptations " (i. 6) ; to suffer for righteousness' sake (iii. 14) ; they are reproached " for the

[1] iv. 12.   [2] *v.* Luke xxiii. 49.   [3] ii. 25.

name of Christ " (iv. 14)—but no man need be ashamed of that, only if he is a " murderer or thief or evil-doer " (iv. 15). It seems that they were subject to slander, to violence, to ostracism such as was the lot of the Christian society everywhere (v. 9). The State was becoming suspicious of the Christian brotherhood as a treasonable society; therefore the readers are to show their loyalty and patriotism so as to put to silence the ignorance of foolish men (ii. 15); to consider the resources of their faith, and especially that " living hope " which looks for an " inheritance incorruptible, and un-defiled, and that fadeth not away . . ." (i. 4, 5).

But others affirm that the fiery trial and the re-proach for the Name [1] must refer to a time when the profession of their religion made the Christians liable to arrest and condemnation. After the exe-cution of Paul by Nero, A.D. 62, " the profession of the Name would have at once become *in law* a penal offence," says Streeter. Peter might then have written warning the Christians in Asia Minor against the trial that was imminent before the per-secution of A.D. 64. But more likely the profes-sion of the Name was not a danger until Nero's outburst. If, then, Peter was himself martyred in that persecution, he must have written this between

---

[1] iv. 12–14.

A.D. 64 and 68. Would he in that case have urged obedience to the State as in ii. 13 ff. ?

For this reason many think the reference is to a date in Domitian's reign, A.D. 90–96, and others to a time as late as the reign of Trajan, since the status of the Christians is similar to that in the letters of Pliny.

On the whole it seems that the persecution is rather that of a general nature. There is no hint that Christians were obliged to worship the emperor as in Domitian's reign; and the attitude of this epistle is very different from that of the Apocalypse to the civil power.

Nor is it clear that it is a crime to be a Christian as in Trajan's reign. Therefore the date in Nero's reign is not unreasonable, and if so, it supports the traditional authorship.

The apocalyptic element is marked, and is consistent with the Petrine authorship. So is the greeting from the Church in Rome. " She that is in Babylon, elect together with *you*, saluteth you : and *so doth* Mark my son " (v. 13). Babylon is part of the apocalyptic vocabulary with which he was familiar. He does not thereby think of Rome as the " mother of harlots." Why should he ?

Significance of the Message. The author writes to encourage those who are enduring trial by giving them a reason for the hope that is in them.[1] That hope was begotten by the resurrection of Jesus Christ from the dead.[2] The readers have tasted that the Lord is gracious, they are " an elect race, a royal priesthood, a holy nation." [3] Therefore they are so to live that those who falsely call them evil-doers may by seeing their good works glorify God. They are to be good and loyal citizens. Slaves are to be obedient, even to those masters who are cruel, following in the footsteps of Christ, the " Shepherd and Bishop of their souls." [4] As himself their pastor he reminds wives and husbands that they are joint-heirs of the grace of life,[5] a grace that is possible for all who are willing to be loving as brethren, repaying reviling with blessing.[6] They will learn what blessedness means, if they should suffer for righteousness' sake.[7] For Christ suffered for sins to bring us to God. And the Cross " has a meaning for all worlds wherever men may be." [8] Let them rejoice to become sharers of Christ's sufferings now ; all the more will they rejoice when they see the revelation of His glory.

He called himself an Apostle at the beginning. At the end he writes : I, who am an elder, exhort you,

---

[1] iii. 15. [2] i. 3. [3] ii. 9. [4] ii. 25.
[5] iii. 7. [6] iii. 8, 9. [7] iii. 14.
[8] *v.* iii. 19, iv. 6.

who are elders, to be loyal in your pastoral office,
and you who are younger to gird yourselves with
humility, that God may exalt you in due time.[1]

"The temper inculcated" by the writer "in
view of suffering is not a grey, close-lipped stoicism,
but a glow of exultation such as Jesus[2] and Paul[3]
had already counselled. Christians can only be
patient under their trials by being more than
patient" (Moffatt).

[1] v. 1-5.   [2] Matt. v. 11 ff.   [3] Rom. v. 3 ff.

CHAPTER XV

THE EPISTLE OF JUDE

Literary Affinities. This short epistle, with a few verbal changes, has been incorporated almost wholly in 2 Peter. Jude 4–16 in 2 Pet. ii. 1–18; Jude 17 ff. in 2 Pet. iii. 2 ff. Mayor thus sums up the literary relationship between them. "In Jude we have the first thought, in 2 Peter the second. We can generally see a reason why 2 Peter should have altered Jude, very rarely a reason why what we read in 2 Peter should have been altered to what we find in Jude. 2 Peter is more reflective, Jude more spontaneous."

Jude seems to be quoting Jewish apocalypses— the Assumption of Moses and the Book of Enoch (9, 14 ff.), books which were probably written in the early part of the first century and were widely read.

There are reminiscences in his book of the Epistles of Paul, e.g. the use of the word ψυχικός, sensual (ver. 19, cf. 1 Cor. ii. 14).[1] The doxology (24, 25) is similar to that of Rom. xvi. 25–27.

---

[1] Cf. τοῖς ἐν θεῷ πατρὶ ἠγαπημένοις Jude 1; ἀδελφοὶ ἠγαπημένοι ὑπὸ τοῦ θεοῦ 1 Thess. i. 4. Cf. 2 Thess. ii. 13.

Ver. 17 ff. are reminiscent of Paul's speech at Miletus (Acts xx. 29 ff.). There are points of affinity with the Didache, which suggest that both had their origin in the same circle.

Canonicity. Considering its brevity, the epistle is well authenticated. It is used, as we have seen, extensively by the author of 2 Peter. It is the only one of the Catholic Epistles, except the Johannine, to be mentioned without doubt in the Muratorian Fragment. Tertullian, Clement of Alexandria, and Origen quote it. But Eusebius puts it among the disputed books—perhaps because of the use it makes of apocalyptic Jewish works, which were in his day regarded with suspicion.

The Author and his Message. The writer calls himself " Judas, a servant of Jesus Christ, and brother of James." Presumably the Jude and James referred to are the brothers of our Lord.[1] Eusebius quotes Hegesippus for the tradition that about A.D. 85 two grandsons of Jude were brought before Domitian as descendants of David and possibly claimants to the throne; and that Jude had been dead for some time. Jude was so obscure, that it seems unlikely that anyone would have composed a letter pseudonymously in his name. But while it might be expected that he would not

---

[1] Mark vi. 3.

call himself " brother of the Lord," it would not have been expected that in a letter which would be carried by hand, and the author of which could be verified by the bearer, the author would describe himself as " brother of James." If we suspect this as a gloss, added when the identity of the Jude was forgotten, the suspicion is confirmed by one or two facts about the epistle.

The author writes as if the apostolic age was already past. " Remember ye the words which have been spoken before by the apostles of our Lord Jesus Christ; how that they said to you, In the last time there shall be mockers. . . ."[1] The writer appears to think he is living in that which the Apostle described as the last time. Again, "the faith which was once for all delivered unto the saints "[2] suggests the writer belongs at least to the second generation of Christians or later.

He appears to have been writing a letter " about our common salvation," [2] when he heard disquieting news. Ungodly men had crept into the Church who deny our only Master and Lord, Jesus Christ. Apparently they were men who defended gross licentiousness as the expression of the liberty which they claimed, because of their possession of a higher

[1] ver. 17.　　　　[2] ver. 3.

and secret knowledge of spiritual things. This
was characteristic of the sect of Carpocrates, who
flourished about A.D. 130. And some scholars
suppose Jude is referring to this sect, for whom
salvation was by magic.

It seems as if this false teaching has only just
crept into the Church to which Jude writes, and it
is the immoral side of it which causes him to de-
nounce it, rather than the falsity of its doctrine. It
need not have been more than a rudimentary form
of Gnosticism, and the heresy seems similar in
some respects to such heresies as were attacked
in the letters to the Seven Churches and in the
Pastoral Epistles. We need not suppose a date
later than about the first decade of the second
century.

If this date is right, then Jude, the brother of our
Lord, cannot be the author—he seems to have died
A.D. 70–80—nor can Judas, the apostle, for he was
the son of James [1] rather than brother. Streeter
thinks there was a bishop of Jerusalem of that name
early in Trajan's reign, and that he may be the
author.[2] Whoever the author be, his attitude to
the heresy is like that of the writer of the Pastorals,
—he denounces rather than refutes by argument, as

[1] Luke vi. 16.
[2] The Primitive Church, pp. 178–180.

Paul would have done. That his epistle is not without its value to-day is shown by the number of phrases from it which have become household words, and from the use that has been made of its doxology.

CHAPTER XVI

THE SECOND EPISTLE OF PETER

Canonicity. The early evidence for the epistle is very doubtful. Clement of Alexandria seems to regard it as the companion of the Apocalypse of Peter[1] rather than of 1 Peter. It is not mentioned in the Muratorian Fragment. Origen alludes to it, but recognizes doubts about it. In the Western Church there is little trace of it before Jerome and Augustine. Eusebius classes it among the *antilegomena.* " The tradition received of us is that it is not canonical; nevertheless, since it appeared profitable to many, store was set by it along with the other Scriptures." [2]

Authorship and Date. Unlike 1 Peter, this epistle lacks most of the marks of a letter at the beginning and at the end. The author calls himself Simon Peter.[3] He seems to go out of his way to refer to his presence at the Transfiguration.[4] He refers to the death of Peter as foretold by Jesus.[5] It may be that he refers to the Gospel of Mark, which, accord-

[1] M. R. James has collected the fragments of this in *The Apocryphal New Testament*, pp. 505–521.
[2] *Hist. Eccles*, iii. 3. [3] i. 1. [4] i. 16,
[5] John xxi. 18, 19 ; 2 Pet. i. 14.

ing to tradition, was derived from Peter's reminiscences.[1] The impression is that the writer stresses his identity unduly. The letter is addressed very vaguely " to them that have obtained a like precious faith with us in the righteousness of our God and Saviour Jesus Christ." [2]

The epistle itself justifies the doubt which the Church felt about its authorship. For there are many evidences that it is the latest book in the New Testament. It seems that Paul's letters were already collected and were classed with the other Scriptures, i.e. of the Old Testament.[3] The first generation of Christians had died. " Where is the promise of His coming? for, from the day that the fathers fell asleep, all things continue as they were from the beginning of the creation." [4] The reference to the Apostle's death [5] might imply that the author knew the Fourth Gospel. If the affinity with the Apocalypse of Peter counts for anything, it suggests both belong to the same time, that is the second century.

The way in which the author has incorporated Jude in his work clearly makes it later than that epistle, and that again puts it in the second century. Attempts are made to prove Jude borrowed from

---

[1] i. 12. [2] i. 1. [3] iii. 16. [4] iii. 4.
[5] i. 14. John xxi. 18, 19.

this letter, but they are not convincing. To meet the difficulty of the epistle's late reception, it is suggested that it had no wide circulation because it was written for Jews ; because of its brevity and the limited interest of its message ; because of the predominance of the Pauline writings. But these things do not explain why a letter supposed to be written by Peter should not have been mentioned by early writers, and should have remained almost unknown till the fourth century.

The literary style is equally against the traditional authorship. The wording is ambitious, artificial, and often obscure : it is the one book in the New Testament which gains by translation. There could hardly be a greater contrast in style than between this and 1 Peter. Is it likely that Peter would have written a letter like this to Jews or Gentiles, where there is no mention of our Lord's Resurrection and Ascension ; no reference to His example (so stressed in 1 Peter) ; no word about the Holy Spirit ?[1] All the evidence points to a date in the middle of the second century for the composition of this book, and makes it impossible to accept the Apostle as the author.

Purpose. The false teaching which the author

---

[1] Except i. 21, and that is in reference to the Old Testament.

denounces in no measured terms is clearly both (a) antinomian, and (b) anti-eschatological.

(a) The first is met in other books of the New Testament, and the writer uses the words of Jude to describe those who preach it. " They bring in destructive heresies, denying even the Master that bought them, bringing upon themselves swift destruction."[1]   " Daring and selfwilled,"[2] he describes them—" children of cursing "[3]—" springs without water."[4]   They promise liberty to those whom they entice, while they themselves are slaves of corruption.[5] They encourage the belief that Christian freedom means freedom from the moral law. Apparently they claimed Paul as their authority, and the author recognizes that there are " some things hard to be understood in his letters, which the ignorant and unstedfast wrest, as *they do* also the other scriptures, unto their own destruction."[6]   But their wickedness is such that the fate of Sodom and Gomorrah will be theirs.[7]

(b) But those who so wantonly outrage Christian liberty no longer believe in a judgment to come. " Where is the promise of his coming " ? they sarcastically ask : " for, from the day that the fathers

---

[1] ii. 1.   [2] ii. 10.   [3] ii. 14.   [4] ii. 17.
[5] ii. 19.   [6] iii. 16.   [7] ii. 6.

fell asleep, all things continue as they were from the beginning of the creation." [1]

This type of heresy and the writer's way of denouncing it remind us of the Pastoral Epistles (2 Tim. iii. 1 ff.; Titus i. 10 ff.). But it is clear that by using Jude's earlier writing, the author is dealing with a situation similar to that which caused Jude to write, and the heresy is like that in Apoc. ii. 2, 6, 9, 13, iii. 4, 8.

Message. The writer's object was to controvert the dangerous teachers of the time, and to do it more effectively by surrounding the appearing of his book with a certain mystery, and by stamping the authority of the Apostle upon it. If we wonder how in the end such a book became one of those in the Canon, the answer is that, since such destructive heresies were a serious menace to the Church, a writing of this religious merit and of uncompromising hostility to such false doctrine was most valuable, especially when it had upon it the name of Peter. Streeter suggests that an additional reason was that " Peter, as well as Paul and John, should be represented in the Canon by a plurality of epistles." [2]

In two respects at least the epistle has a word in season for this age. It reminds those who advocate

[1] iii. 4.   [2] *The Primitive Church*, p. 191.

licence in the name of freedom that " a man is the slave of whatever overpowers him." [1]

The writer believed that the Flood ended one world, and that fire will dissolve this in the Day of Judgment. He reminds those who say that " all things continue as they were from the beginning of the creation " that God is very patient, His apparent inactivity is due to His long-suffering, "not wishing that any should perish, but that all should come to repentance." [2] " Seeing that these things are thus all to be dissolved, what manner of persons ought ye to be in *all* holy living and godliness, looking for and earnestly desiring the coming of the day of God . . . (which is to in-augurate) new heavens and a new earth, wherein dwelleth righteousness." [3]

[1] ii. 19 (Moffatt).   [2] iii. 9.   [3] iii. 11-13.

PART V

THE SYNOPTIC GOSPELS AND ACTS

CHAPTER XVII

THE SYNOPTIC PROBLEM

The first three Gospels are called Synoptic because they give a common view of the life of our Lord and are similar in the general scheme and in the selection of material. The resemblances between them are more marked when they are compared with the Fourth Gospel. (*a*) In the Fourth Gospel, apart from the story of the Passion and the Resurrection, there is an almost entirely different selection of facts. The Feeding of the Five Thousand is the only narrative common to the four Gospels. (*b*) The Fourth Gospel presents a different view of our Lord's Ministry. According to this Gospel He made many journeys between Jerusalem and Galilee, but spent the greater part of the time in Jerusalem. In the Synoptic Gospels no account is given of any visit to Jerusalem until the last week. (*c*) The discourses of the Lord are quite different in character in the first three Gospels from those recorded in the Fourth. This applies to the controversy with the Jews and to the teaching of the disciples.

On the other hand, there is a striking amount of agreement between the Synoptic Gospels. (*a*)

They have a large common element in the narratives and discourses. Mark has been divided into 105 sections, and only 4 of these are absent both from Matthew and from Luke. Of the remaining 101 sections, 93 are found in Matthew and 81 in Luke. Although there are large portions of Matthew and Luke not found in Mark, there is much that is common to the two Evangelists in these portions. (b) After the account of the Baptism and the Temptation the general scheme of these three Gospels is identical. The Ministry begins and continues in Galilee or a little farther north, until the journey to Jerusalem which precedes the Passion. And within the scheme there is a general similarity of order, particularly in those sections which are found in the three Gospels. (c) The agreement is not only in the general scheme and in the order of events, but is found in the very words with which the story is told. This is the more remarkable when it is remembered that our Lord would have spoken in Aramaic as a rule, and in that language, for some time at any rate, His words and the accounts of His works would have been related.

To explain this agreement some literary connexion between the three has been supposed from very early times. The simplest assumption was

that one used another, e.g. that Mark cut down
Matthew as Augustine thought,[1] but that will
hardly account for all the facts. The many modern
theories which have been put forward in the last
one hundred and fifty years may be classed under
two heads—(*a*) documentary, (*b*) oral.

(*a*) According to the Documentary Hypothesis
there was one primitive Gospel—Urevangelium—
to which various additions derived from oral
teaching were made from time to time.

(*b*) According to the Oral Hypothesis the three
Evangelists used an oral tradition which had obtained a high degree of fixity. There is no doubt
that ultimately the Gospels do go back to oral
teaching, and the requirements of that teaching
determined the general selection of the facts and
discourses which they relate. The question is
whether our written Gospels rest directly on this
oral teaching, or whether other documents came
between which have now been lost. The great
advantage of this hypothesis is that it escapes the
difficulty of inventing documents the existence of
which must always be difficult to prove; and we
know that it was in accordance with Jewish custom
to learn by heart long strings of connected sayings
of the Rabbis and hand them down from mouth

[1] Pedisequus et breviator Matthaei.

to mouth from one generation to another. But on this hypothesis agreement would have been expected at the critical points of our Lord's Ministry, whereas, in fact, the most remarkable instances of it are in quite unimportant details : in the narrative of the Passion and the Resurrection, where closest agreement would be expected, there are remarkable differences. Therefore, while the formation of the oral tradition behind the written Gospels forms one of the most recent studies in Gospel origins, the explanation of the Synoptic problem which is almost universally held to-day is the Documentary Hypothesis.

The Documentary Hypothesis. This has assumed many different forms since Eichhorn supposed one primitive Gospel from which the others were derived. Almost all scholars are now agreed that there are two main documents underlying the first three Gospels : (1) Mark, in its present or possibly slightly different form ; (2) another document, consisting of sayings and discourses of our Lord, used by both Matthew and Luke. This is called Q.[1]

---

[1] Q was apparently first used as a symbol by Armitage Robinson in lectures at Cambridge to distinguish the sayings-document from P, the reminiscences of Peter. It then appeared in Wellhausen's *Einleitung* and was understood as the first letter of the German word for source— *Quelle.* *v.* R. H. Lightfoot, *History and Interpretation in the Gospels,* pp. 27, 28.

(1) *Mark as the source of Matthew and Luke.*

The evidence for the priority of Mark is :

1. Almost all Mark is contained in Matthew or Luke or in both. It seems to follow that either Mark is compiled from the other two, or that they used Mark. A detailed comparison of the texts shows that the former view is untenable. Take, for example, the Healing of the Paralytic.[1] If the three narratives are compared, it will be seen that after the introduction, which is peculiar to each Evangelist, there is nothing in Matthew and Luke which is not found in Mark, but Mark has much pictorial detail which is wanting in the other two. It is hardly possible that Mark should have compiled his narrative from the other two, and yet should be the freshest and most lifelike of the three. In this, and similar parallel sections, it is noteworthy that the majority of the actual words used by Mark are reproduced by Matthew and Luke, either alternately or both together.

2. The relative order of events in Mark is, generally speaking, supported by the other two Gospels. Thus if Mark is divided into three arbitrary sections —(1) i. 1–iii. 6, (2) iii. 7–vi. 13, (3) vi. 14–xvi. 8—in (1) the order is practically identical with Luke ; in (3) with that of Matthew, and to a less extent

[1] Mark ii. 1–12 ; Luke v. 17–26 ; Matt. ix. 1–8.

with that of Luke; (2) is more broken up, but here, too, the order of Mark has alternately the support of either Matthew or Luke.

The similarity of Matthew or Luke or both with Mark in the content, the order, and even the words, can only be explained satisfactorily if they are incorporating a source practically identical with Mark.

3. The primitive character of Mark is seen, in that phrases which might be misunderstood are absent from the parallel passages in Matthew and Luke. It seems as if Matthew and Luke deliberately omitted or changed such words, just as they improved Mark's grammar and phraseology, and omitted most of his Aramaic words. Mark is rougher in style, the others are more literary. Mark probably reproduces the primitive tradition more accurately—e.g. Mark does not use " the Lord " (ὁ κύριος) of Jesus,[1] Matthew uses it nineteen times, and Luke sixteen.

4. Canon Streeter has noted that the way in which Markan and non-Markan material is distributed in Matthew and Luke respectively makes it probable that each had before him the Markan material in a single document, and was faced with the problem of combining this with material from other sources. Matthew makes the Markan outline the framework, into which is fitted the material

---

[1] Mark xi. 3 may be no exception.

derived from other sources ; Luke, except in the Passion narrative, sets the Markan and non-Markan material in alternate blocks.

Did Matthew and Luke use our Mark or an Ur-Markus?   If Matthew and Luke used our Mark, why (1) do they omit certain sections ? (2) do they agree in minute verbal expressions against Mark ? Had they an earlier edition than Mark as we know it ?

1. Matthew omits in all only fifty-five verses of Mark, and Luke has twenty-four of these. But the omission in Luke of Mark vi. 45–viii. 26, containing among other things the story of the Syro-Phoenician Woman, has raised the question whether the author of Luke used a copy of Mark in which this section was not found. A more likely explanation is that the author of Luke preferred his non-Markan source, and that had somewhat similar incidents, as Streeter and Vincent Taylor suggest. Or, as J. M. Creed thinks, the author of Luke may have regarded some of the incidents in this section of Mark as doublets, and have rejected the story of the Syro-Phoenician Woman as a stumbling-block to the Gentiles. In any case, the authors of the First and Third Gospels were historians who had a right to select their material.

2. Most of the small verbal agreements of

Matthew and Luke against Mark are of little importance. Possibly the text of Mark which they used had been slightly revised, and our text is the unrevised and earlier—the opposite to the Ur-Markus theory.

(2) *The source called Q.*

Matthew and Luke have in common material, not found in Mark, amounting to rather more than 200 verses. This includes the account of the Preaching of the Baptist, the details of the Temptation, the Sermon on the Mount, the Healing of the Centurion's Servant, the Question asked by the Baptist, and very many of the most noteworthy Sayings in the Gospels. But this common material does not occur in the same contexts or in the same order in many cases in the two Gospels. And sometimes the verbal resemblances are very close—e.g. in the Denunciation by the Baptist of the Pharisees and Sadducees[1]; but at other times the contrast is greater than the resemblances—e.g. in the number and the form of the Beatitudes.[2] There are three possible explanations : (*a*) Matthew used Luke, or Luke Matthew. This seems unlikely, because, after the story of the Temptation, the two do not agree in inserting the same saying at the same point in the

---

[1] Matt. iii. 7–10 ; Luke iii. 7–9.
[2] Matt. v. 3–12 ; Luke vi. 20–23.

Markan outline. And sometimes it is the one, and sometimes it is the other, who quotes the saying in what is clearly its more original form. (*b*) The two Evangelists made use of different cycles of oral tradition. But that hardly explains the cases where the verbal resemblances are very close and remarkable—e.g. the Baptist's Denunciation (*c*) Matthew and Luke both made use of a single document which has been lost—the document Q.

Can Q be Reconstructed? (1) It would not be possible to reconstruct Mark, if it had been lost, seeing that less than two-thirds of it is contained in both Matthew and Luke. Therefore it is likely that only a part of Q has been preserved in the non-Markan matter common to Matthew and Luke. Other parts of Q will be preserved in sections peculiar to Matthew or Luke, but it will be difficult to identify them. (2) Where the same sayings are recorded in slightly different form, Matthew and Luke may have derived them from oral tradition, and not from Q at all. (3) Those sections in which the order is much the same may be taken to give a skeleton of Q. In the other sections common to both Luke's order is more likely to reproduce that of Q than Matthew's, because he seems to keep more closely to the Markan order than Matthew, who groups sayings on similar topics into long discourses. Further, if the original order of Q is better represented in Luke than in Matthew, then certain short passages in Q contexts found in Luke, but not in Matthew, may be from Q.—e.g. Luke vi. 24–26, ix. 61–62, xii. 35–38.

Many attempts have been made to reconstruct Q. The following is the list of passages which Streeter [1] assigns to Q. The parallels from Matthew are added :

1. The Baptist and the Baptism of Jesus : Luke iii. 2–9 (10–14), 16–17, 21–22 ; Matt. iii. 7–12, 16–17.

2. The Temptation and Appearance in Galilee : Luke iv. 1–16a ; Matt. iv. 1–11.

3. The Sermon on the Plain and the Centurion's Servant : Luke vi. 20–vii. 10 ; Matt. v. 3, 4, 6, 11, 12, 44, vii. (*passim*), viii. 5–10, 13, and Sayings elsewhere reported.

4. The Baptist's Question, and the Witness of Jesus to the Baptist : Luke vii. 18–35 ; Matt. xi. 2–11, 16–19.

5. The Journey to Jerusalem, Would-be Disciples : Luke ix. (51–56), ix. 57–60 (61–62) ; Matt. viii. 19–22.

6. The Mission of the Seventy : Luke x. 2–16

---

[1] *The Four Gospels*, p. 291.

(17–20), 21–24; Matt. ix. 37–38, x. 16, 10–13, xi. 25–27, xiii. 16–17.

7. Various Sayings, Defence against the Beelzebub Charge: Luke xi. 9–52; Matt. vii. 7–11, xii. 22–27, 43–45, 38–42, v. 15, vi. 22–23, xxiii (*passim*).

8. Warnings against fears, cares, etc.: Luke xii. 1a–12, 22–59; Matt. x. 26–33, xii. 32, vi. 25–33, 19–21, xxiv. 43–51, x. 34–36, v. 25–26.

9. Parables of the Mustard Seed, Leaven, etc.: Luke xiii. 18–35; Matt. xiii. 31–33, vii. 13, viii. 11–12, xxiii. 37–39.

10. Warnings to the Disciples: Luke xiv. 11, 26–27, 34–35; Matt. x. 37–38, v. 13.

11. The Law and Divorce: Luke xvi. 13, 16–18; Matt. vi. 24, xi. 12–13, v. 18, 32.

12. Warnings against causing others to stumble, etc.: Luke xvii. 1–6, 20–37; Matt. xviii. 6–7, 15, 21–22, xvii. 20, xxiv (*passim*).

13. The Parable of the Pounds: Luke xix. 11–27; Matt. xxv. 14–30.

The unbracketed verses number 272. The brackets signify that there is some doubt about the verses so marked.

From this it will be clearly seen that the document called Q was principally discourse : the only narrative as such in it seems to have been that of the Centurion's Servant. It was probably a selection

of those words of Jesus which were most suitable to
give guidance to those engaged in the Christian
Mission in the Apostolic age. They needed to
have answers to the questions, How was the Gospel
related to the Baptist and his message ? What was
the attitude of the Lord to the Pharisees and to the
Law ? It may be taken as certain that Q had no
account of the Passion, because, although Luke
seems independent of Mark in much of his Passion
narrative, there is no substantial agreement of
Matthew and Luke against Mark there. In all
probability Q was meant to supplement an oral
tradition, but it made no pretensions to be a
Gospel. The story of the Cross was too familiar
to need a supplement.

Mark and Q. The opinions of scholars are
divided, but there is good ground for thinking
that Mark did not know Q. The sections common to both cover about fifty verses : the Preaching of the Baptist; the Baptism ; the Temptation ;
the Beelzebub Controversy ; the Sending out of the
Disciples ; the Woes on the Pharisees. Since it is
Matthew's custom to combine Mark and Q, it is
fairer to compare Mark with Luke's version of Q,
and the differences are striking. In the account
of the Temptation [1] and of the Sending out of the

---

[1] Mark i. 12, 13 ; Luke iv. 1–13.

Disciples[1] the differences are so great, and the resemblances are so few, that it seems unlikely there is any literary dependence of the one upon the other. If Mark had known and used Q, he would hardly have left his story of the Temptation as it is. It might be that Mark knew Q in another recension than that used by Matthew and Luke; or he may have written to supplement Q; but the evidence rather suggests that he did not use Q at all.

Proto-Luke. There is much in Luke not derived either from Mark or Q. The beginning and the end of the Gospel are non-Markan. In the account of the Preaching of the Baptist, the Baptism, and the Temptation Luke seems to be following Q, not Mark. Luke's narrative of the Passion is mainly, and of the Resurrection wholly, derived from another source than Mark or Q, for Q had no Passion narrative. In the middle of the Gospel there are three large sections which are non-Markan: (1) vi. 12–viii. 3, sometimes called the *Lesser Interpolation*; (2) ix. 51–xviii. 14, the *Great Interpolation*; (3) xix. 1–28. It is asked, Is not the word *Interpolation* a misnomer here? Is not the Markan matter rather an *Interpolation* in a non-Markan framework?

The non-Markan matter in Luke is derived partly from Q and partly from L, a symbol to denote a

[1] Mark vi. 7–11; Luke x. 1–12.

source peculiar to the Third Gospel. It appears that, where Mark and Q overlap, the writer of the Gospel prefers Q, as in the story of the Temptation; and where Mark and L overlap, as in the narrative of the Passion, Luke prefers L. If Q and L were already combined so that they already formed a Gospel and were in Luke's possession before he read Mark, then it would account for his preference for his non-Markan framework much more satisfactorily than if he had Mark, Q, and L all separate before him. That Q and L had been combined into one document and were the principal foundation of the Third Gospel is the Proto-Luke theory. This was first put forward by Streeter in an article in the *Hibbert Journal* in 1921 and enlarged by him in *The Four Gospels*. The arguments in favour of the theory and the very important inferences to be drawn from it were most carefully investigated by Vincent Taylor in *Behind the Third Gospel*. The following is Vincent Taylor's reconstruction of what he well calls the " First Draft " of the Gospel, i.e. Proto-Luke.

1. iii. 1–iv. 30. The Preaching of the Baptist, Baptism, Genealogy, Temptation, Departure to Galilee, Sermon at Nazareth.

2. v. 1–11. Call of Simon.

---

1 Vincent Taylor, *The First Draft of St. Luke's Gospel* (S.P.C.K.).

3. vi. 12–viii. 3.   Choice of Apostles, Miracles, Great Sermon, Centurion's Servant, Widow of Nain, Message of Baptist, Woman who was a Sinner, Preaching Tour.

4. ix. 51–xviii. 14.   Journey to Jerusalem, the Seventy, Good Samaritan, Martha and Mary, the Lord's Prayer, Beelzebub Controversy, Sign of Jonah, Woes, Rich Fool, Sundry Sayings and Parables—Great Supper, Lost Coin, Lost Sheep, Lost Son, Unjust Steward, Dives and Lazarus, Unjust Judge, Pharisee and Publican.

5. xix. 1–28.   Zacchaeus, Parable of Pounds.

6. xix. 37–44, 47–48.   Lament over Jerusalem, etc.

7. xxii. 14–xxiv. 53 (less the Markan additions). The Last Supper, Agony, Arrest, Mocking, Trial before Priests—before Pilate—before Herod— before Pilate (resumed), Journey to the Cross, Crucifixion, Visit of Women to Tomb, Emmaus, Appearance to the Eleven, Parting.

" The style, treatment, and characteristic ideas of Proto-Luke stamp this document as the work of Luke himself " (Vincent Taylor).[1]   It is most probable that Luke wrote a travel diary which he used some years afterwards in writing the latter half of Acts.   The writer of that diary stayed in the house

[1] *The Gospels*, p. 45.

of Philip in Caesarea.[1]   Philip was the Evangelist of
Samaria (Acts viii. 4 ff.).   In Proto-Luke there is a
special interest in Samaria and in the Samaritans.[2]
Caesarea was the capital of the Herod dynasty, and
the writer of Proto-Luke and of Acts had special
knowledge of and interest in the Herods,[3] perhaps
through Chuza [4] and Manaen.[5] It seems most
reasonable to suppose that Luke gathered much of
the material peculiar to his Gospel while he was in
Caesarea, and that later he combined this with
material from Q.   Later still he expanded this first
draft into the Gospel, as we have it, by prefixing
the stories of the Infancy and inserting extracts from
Mark.   The Lukan traits—the gentleness, the interest in the miraculous, and, above all, the presentation of Christ as the Saviour of the world—are
found equally in Proto-Luke as in the rest of the
Gospel and in the Acts.

Although widely accepted, this theory has not
convinced all scholars.   J. M. Creed [6] maintains
that if the Markan material is subtracted from Luke,
the result is " an amorphous collection of narrative
and discourse," which he grants may have been
before Luke in a very loosely constructed single

[1] Acts xxi. 8.   [2] Luke ix. 51–56, x. 25 ff.
[3] Luke xiii. 31–33, xxiii. 8–12.   [4] Luke viii. 3.
[5] Acts xiii. 1.
[6] *The Gospel according to St. Luke*, p. lviii.

document. But he thinks that Luke has drawn material from this and fitted it into his Markan framework, regarding Mark as his primary authority. If this is so, then Luke himself did not attach the importance as historical data to QL, which Streeter and Vincent Taylor claim for it. But, as Vincent Taylor[1] points out, the fact that there is a solid block of non-Markan material (iii. 1–iv. 30) at the beginning of Luke's Gospel (after the Infancy stories); the fact that the differences between the Passion Narrative in Mark and Luke are best explained by the belief that Luke used his non-Markan source as his basic document; the fact that the Markan sections, if taken away from the context in Luke, have no unity in themselves, are strong evidence that Luke preferred QL as a whole, and used it as the framework; and that Mark was for him the later stratum from which he only drew what he considered necessary to expand his own original draft.[2]

The importance of this theory, if true, is that Proto-Luke and Mark are two independent authorities of about the same date. Both are likely to have been later than Q : Proto-Luke was probably written after Luke left Caesarea, A.D. 60–65.[3] As an historical

---

[1] *The Formation of the Gospel Tradition*, pp. 191 ff.

[2] *v. The Expository Times*, vol. xlvi, pp. 101 ff., pp. 236 ff., pp. 256 ff.

[3] Vincent Taylor, *The Gospels*, p. 45 ; but *v.* Streeter, *The Four Gospels*, p. 221.

authority Luke himself regarded Proto-Luke as
equal to Mark. It is reasonable to regard it as an
early and historical work comparable to Mark,
though it is doubtful if we should attach equal
weight to it as to Mark. It may have been revised
to some extent by Luke before he published it in the
form in which we now read it.

Matthew's Special Source. There is material in
Matthew, chiefly discourse and parable, which is
derived neither from Mark nor Q. If this is from
a single source, then it is clear that it represented
traditions parallel to those preserved in Mark, Q,
and L. The Sermon on the Mount in Matthew is
about four times as long as Luke's Sermon on the
Plain. The Sermon in Luke seems to have come
from Q, and Matthew has added to it Q material
found in other contexts in Luke. But when these
sections are abstracted, two-thirds of the Sermon in
Matthew are left, and the whole reads like a continuous discourse, which would have been a larger
Sermon than that in Q, and which Matthew has
collated with the Sermon and other material from
Q. Similarly, Matthew has collated Q (Luke xi.
37–52) with another parallel discourse in Matt.
xxiii. 1–36. A comparison of Matt. xix. 3–12 with
Mark x. 2–12, of Matt. xii. 9–13 with Mark iii. 1–6,
and of Matt. xv. 22b–24 with Mark vii. 24–30 shows

that in our Lord's words upon the questions of Divorce, the observance of the Sabbath, and the admission of the Gentiles (the Syro-Phoenician Woman), Matthew had another source which, as was his custom, he collated with Mark. That this was a written source cannot be proved; Matthew may have been using oral tradition or a group of sources. But that M, as Streeter calls it, does represent a tradition distinct from Q, though in some ways parallel to it, whether M was written or oral, is a much more satisfactory explanation than to account for the resemblances and the differences between Matthew and Luke by saying that they used different recensions of Q; for that would mean that only about half of Q as Matthew knew it was identical with half of the same document as Luke knew it. Passages which may be assigned to M are:

1. The Sermon on the Mount—the relation of the New Dispensation to the Law (v. 17–39); Religious Observances (vi. 1–18).

2. The parables peculiar to Matthew: Tares, Hid Treasure, Pearl of Great Price, Draw-net, Unmerciful Servant, Labourers in the Vineyard, Two Sons, Marriage of the King's Son, Ten Virgins, Sheep and Goats, and probably the parables, which are also in Luke, Lost Sheep, Marriage Feast, Talents.

3. The parts of Matt. xxiii. which are not parallel to Luke xi. 37–52.

4. Sayings about Divorce, etc., to which reference has already been made, and others such as xiii. 52, xvi. 17–19, xviii. 15–22, xix. 28.

Whether M was a written or oral source, it is from M that the Judaistic passages are derived, and that gives ground for thinking that, as Streeter suggests, M represents the traditions of the Church of Jerusalem. It is to be expected that the traditions of that Church would have been incorporated in one of our four Gospels, and " M is the kind of collection we should expect to emanate from Jerusalem " (Streeter).[1]

The stories of the Nativity, of Peter walking on the Water, of the Stater in the Fish's Mouth, and those connected with the Passion which are peculiar to Matthew's Gospel, which have some special knowledge of Judas and of Pilate, etc., are not from M, but emanate from an oral cycle of tradition in all probability current in the Church for which this Gospel was written.[2]

The Four-document Hypothesis. This has led Streeter[3] to postulate a " Four-document Hypothesis " for the former " Two-document " explana-

---

[1] *The Four Gospels*, pp. 254 ff.　　[2] *Ibid.*, p. 266.
[3] *Ibid.*, p. 268.

tion of the Synoptic Problem. Each of the four documents represents the traditions of an important Church. Mark was the Gospel of the Church in Rome ; L is connected with Caesarea ; M probably with Jerusalem. Q, since it was important enough to have been used by both Luke and Matthew, would be likely to have represented the traditions of an important Church. It was probably written in Aramaic, and was certainly Palestinian in origin, but it had been translated into Greek before Matthew and Luke used it. Its missionary interest, and the inclusion in it of such passages as Luke xvi. 16, " The law and the prophets *were* until John : from that time the gospel of the kingdom of God is preached, and every man entereth violently into it," and of Matt. viii. 10, " I have not found so great faith, no, not in Israel," are adduced by Streeter to support his conjecture that Q was connected with the Church of Antioch. There is good reason for thinking that the First Gospel was written in Antioch, and some evidence that Luke was an Antiochene,[1] and the writers of both the First and Third Gospels we know used Q.

Streeter thus explains how our four Gospels came into being, how they were preserved in the Church,

[1] Acts xi. 28. The Bezan text reads : " And when *we* were assembled together."

and how there is so little authentic tradition found outside these four. Mark, though practically incorporated in Matthew and Luke, was the Gospel of the Church in Rome. Matthew represents the traditions of Rome (Mark), Antioch (Q), Jerusalem (M); Luke the traditions of Rome (Mark), Antioch (Q), Caesarea (L). The Fourth Gospel records the tradition vouched for by the Church at Ephesus. " The connexion of these Gospels with the great Churches explains the authoritative position which, as against all rivals, they soon achieved, and thus their ultimate selection as the nucleus of the Canon. It was because the Synoptic Gospels included what each of the great Churches most valued in its own local traditions, and much more also, that the records of these local traditions were allowed to perish." [1]

Form-criticism. The Form-historical Method, in which the pioneer was Martin Dibelius, who in 1919 published *Die Formgeschichte des Evangeliums*, is an investigation of the oral tradition which has received literary form in the Gospels. It assumes that in the oral period the tradition circulated in separate units which can be classified according to their form. It describes the history of these pre-literary forms, what may be inferred about the origin of the units, how they came to be grouped together, and the

---

[1] *The Four Gospels*, p. 269.

changes which they underwent, before they assumed the written form in which we know them. The separate units are classified into groups, the most obvious of which are sayings and narratives. But the exponents of this method are not content with analysis. They pass historical judgments upon the groups and the units, and then Form-history becomes Form-criticism, which is the name most commonly used in English. There is no agreed terminology about the groups. Paradigms (Dibelius), Apophthegms (Bultmann), Pronouncement-stories (Vincent Taylor), refer to similar though not the same groups. The names of others, such as Miracles, Myths, Legends, not only classify but pass historical judgments upon the forms. This school attempts further to recover the original forms in cases where the saying or narrative is found in the written Gospels in a secondary form. It is claimed that these isolated sayings and stories owe their existence and their form to the situation in which the Christians of the earliest days found themselves, to the necessities of the Christian Mission. Bultmann thinks that the Apophthegms came out of debates in the Palestinian communities, so that they are " ideal scenes " which illustrate some principle which the community traced back to Jesus. " The Evangelists were therefore composers and only to the smallest extent authors. They are principally collectors, vehicles of tradition, editors " (Dibelius). The whole framework of the Gospel as we read it is an " editorial construction " (Bultmann). It is true that we have but a small selection of typical scenes from our Lord's life and teaching, no orderly biography or even outline of His ministry. But Vincent Taylor's judgment is a sober estimate of the facts, " the tradition of the words of Jesus is far better preserved than we have any right to expect, and with much greater accuracy than is to be found in the record of the words of any great teacher of the past." [1] While it was the community which made these Paradigms, or whatever they may be called, current, that is quite another thing from saying that the community produced them, as Bultmann maintains. [2] Individuals, not communities, produce striking sayings. And it is not impossible that Jesus Himself taught His disciples to commit to memory the first tradition of the sayings groups and parables. Form-criticism is a valuable method of classifying the material, but in itself it does not enable us to determine the origin of the tradition, or to pass judgment upon its value to the historian. It does, however, help us to see

[1] *The Formation of the Gospel Tradition*, p. 113.
[2] So Loisy in *L'évangile selon Luc*.

the preliterary stages out of which the written Gospels have emerged; and it makes more vivid those incidents in the life of Jesus and His disciples which were first told from mouth to mouth and later repeated whenever the Christians gathered to " break bread " and to pray together, long years before they were written in even the earliest of the documents which underlie the Gospels as we know them.

CHAPTER XVIII

THE GOSPEL ACCORDING TO MARK

Authorship. The Second Gospel was universally assigned by tradition to John Mark, who is mentioned in Acts and in the Epistles eight times, in each case in association with Peter or Paul.[1] Papias, according to Eusebius,[2] says : " The Elder said ' Mark having become the interpreter of Peter wrote down accurately everything that he remembered, without however recording in order what was said or done by Christ. For neither did he hear the Lord, nor did he follow Him ; but afterwards, as I said, attended Peter, who adapted his instructions to the needs of his hearers, but had no design of giving a connected account of the Lord's oracles. So then Mark made no mistake, while he thus wrote down some things as he remembered them ; for he made it his one care not to omit anything that he heard or to set down any false statement therein.' " This is the statement of a contemporary, for John the Elder, whom Papias is quoting, was a disciple of the Lord, one of the followers of the Apostles, as

[1] Acts xii. 12–25, xv. 37, 39 ; Col. iv. 10 ; Philem. 24 ; 2 Tim. iv. 11 ; I Pet. v. 13.
[2] *Hist. Eccles.* iii. 39.

Mark and Luke themselves were.   The Elder does not call Mark's work a gospel, but clearly connects it with the teaching of Peter, who taught according to the needs of his hearers.   The criticism that Mark's book is not a connected account of the Lord's oracles, that he did not " record in order [1] what was said or done by Christ " is not unfair. Streeter [2] thinks John the Elder makes it in order to defend the chronology of the Fourth Gospel which conflicts with Mark in order.   How far later writers are dependent upon Papias is not clear, but Clement of Alexandria, Origen, and Jerome attribute the Gospel to Mark under the influence of Peter. Justin seems to identify it with the " Memoirs of Peter."   And though it left fewer traces than the other Gospels in the early Christian writers, this Gospel was everywhere included in the sacred quaternion of gospels by the end of the second century.

There seems no reason why John Mark should have been universally regarded as the author of the Gospel unless it was true.   He was well known to the leaders of the early Church.   The absence of personal reminiscences (except perhaps xiv. 51, 52 and xv. 21) may be due to his desire to give the Petrine tradition, and to the fact that he is not a

---

[1] οὐ μέντοι τάξει.   [2] *The Four Gospels*, pp. 17 ff.

N.T.—8*

practised author like the authors of the First and
Third Gospels. It is probable that viii. 1–26 is a
duplicate narrative of events related in vi. 31–vii. 37,
and that ch. xiii. incorporates an apocalyptic pamphlet of an earlier date, but these facts do not disprove
that Mark was the author ; they make it clear that
he used other sources besides his remembrance of
the teaching of Peter.

Place and Time of Writing. The earliest tradition
is that Mark wrote his Gospel in Rome [1] for the
Roman Church. (*a*) He is connected with Rome
in 1 Pet. v. 13 and 2 Tim. iv. 11. (*b*) The translation of Aramaic phrases suggests that he wrote
for a Gentile Church, and the use of Latin [2] technical words and phrases supports Rome. (*c*) The
dating of the Last Supper, it is thought, may be
due to the observance of Easter which was familiar
in the Roman Church. (*d*) Streeter claims that
the survival of this Gospel when it was already
incorporated in Matthew and Luke is most easily
explained by its connexion with Rome and with
Peter.

Three dates have been suggested for the composition of the Gospel :

[1] The so-called anti-Marcionite Prologue to this Gospel states that it
was written *in partibus Italiae*, by Mark *interpres Petri*, after the Apostle's
death.

[2] E.g. ξέστης, σπεκουλάτωρ, τὸ ἱκανὸν ποιεῖν.

1. About A.D. 50.   This has the weighty support
of Harnack, but of very few other modern scholars.
Harnack thought Luke wrote Acts before Paul was
martyred, and of course the Third Gospel must
have been written before Acts.   Mark's Gospel,
being one of the sources of the Third Gospel, must
be earlier still.   If Mark's Gospel had been originally written in Aramaic, this date might be possible,
but even so the internal evidence is against it, and
the most probable dating of Acts does not require it.

2. About A.D. 65–66.   Irenaeus says: "After their
deaths Mark, the disciple and interpreter of Peter,
himself also handed down to us in writing the
things which Peter had proclaimed."[1]   It would be
natural that the record of Peter's teaching would
have been made soon after the Apostle's martyrdom.
Clement of Alexandria says that Mark wrote during
Peter's lifetime,[2] but Irenaeus is more likely to be
right.   The freshness of its colouring and the lack
of any indication that Jerusalem has fallen suggest
a date before A.D. 70, when the Temple is still
standing (cf. xiii. 1).   The use the author makes of
the " Little Apocalypse " in ch. xiii, and the probable reference in xiii. 14 to the expected appearance
of Anti-Christ,[3] suggest that the troubles had already

---

[1] *Adv. Haer.* III, i. 2.   [2] Eusebius, *Hist. Eccles.* vi. 14.
[3] ὅταν ἴδητε τὸ βδέλυγμα τῆς ἐρημώσεως ἑστηκότα ὅπου οὐ δεῖ.

begun, and the reader is warned that the sign is near. The references to the persecution which the disciples must expect would be consistent with a date after Peter and Paul and many other Christians had suffered martyrdom in the latter part of Nero's reign.

3. After A.D. 70. (*a*) B. W. Bacon [1] thinks Mark's words about " the abomination of desolation " are studiedly vague because he writes after A.D. 70. But Mark would have been less vague if he had been writing after the prophecy had been fulfilled. (*b*) It is claimed that Mark's dating of the Last Supper reflects the usage of the Roman Church in the Quarto-deciman controversy, and that this divergence could not have arisen until some time after the deaths of Peter and Paul. But the objection is based on an inconclusive conjecture.

Original Language. The style of Mark's Greek is non-literary : his writing lacks connecting particles, is without polish, colloquial, and monotonous. There are a number of Semitisms, Latinisms, stereotyped phrases, and redundancies. Some of the roughnesses are smoothed away in the text of the Alexandrian uncials, but are preserved in the Western text. F. Blass, J. Wellhausen, and C. C. Torrey argue from these peculiarities that the Gospel was originally written in Aramaic, and

[1] *Gospel of Mark*, p. 64.

that what has come to us is a translation, in which
are found many inaccurate renderings. But (a) Matthew and Luke knew Mark's Gospel only in Greek ;
and (b) would a translator have left certain Aramaic
words such as we find in a number of important
passages ?[1] It is not unlikely that Mark used
sources in Aramaic, that he was accustomed to hear
Peter preach in Aramaic. He himself habitually
thought in Aramaic, and was an imperfect Greek
scholar. J. H. Moulton says his Gospel is in
" virtual translation Greek." W. F. Howard calls
it " the most Aramaic of the Gospels." Lagrange,
" His Greek is always Greek, yet translation
Greek ; not that he translates an Aramaic writing,
but because he reproduces an Aramaic κατήχησις.[2]"

Sources. Papias's description of Mark as the
" interpreter of Peter " has not been questioned
until modern times. There is much in the Gospel
which seems to accord with the tradition. Peter
may have been present at all the scenes except at
the Baptism, the Temptation, and the Crucifixion.
Occasionally Peter is identified where Matthew and
Luke are indefinite. Though the style is unpolished,

[1] v. 41, vii. 11, xiv. 36, xv. 22, 34. *v. supra*, p. 184. In almost all
cases of Aramaic words in Mark the translation into Greek follows.
This suggests not a translator but an original Greek writer.

[2] *v.* W. F. Howard in *Grammar of New Testament Greek* (Moulton &
Howard), vol. ii, p. 481.

it is graphic, and there are often words which suggest an eye-witness's account; and the rather loose way in which the vividly told stories are connected is consistent with personal reminiscence. Although many attempts have been made (especially by B. W. Bacon) to find the Pauline theology in Mark's Gospel, the general opinion is that it reflects simple and primitive thought, and while it relates stories of miracles, there is no attempt to heighten them.[1]

But there are other and secondary traits in the Gospel. The writer seems to disparage Peter and the Twelve, and gives Peter less prominence than he has in Matthew. There is little doubt that in ch. xiii a written apocalyptic pamphlet is used, and that in ch. viii is another account of events already recorded in the previous section, the Feeding of the Multitude, etc. If Peter is behind the Evangelist, an account of the Ministry fuller and with more definite chronological sequence would have been expected. The author is suspected of inaccuracy in geographical detail, in speaking of a journey from Tyre through Sidon through Decapolis (vii. 31); in historical fact, in the date of the Crucifixion, and the identification of the Last Supper with the Passover Meal; in the account of the meeting of the whole

[1] J. M. C. Crum in St. Mark's Gospel has attempted to distinguish between two sources—one a simple narrative of facts, the other a later and more theological work.

Sanhedrin in the night of the arrest of the Lord.[1]

It can hardly be claimed that the Gospel is a verbatim account of Peter's preaching, Petro narrante illo scribente, as Jerome says. But much of it reflects the primitive tradition of the Palestinian Church as the Roman Church had received it from Peter himself. Mark, however, has drawn upon other sources, some written, some oral, and some personal, and since he is perhaps the first who is attempting a continuous story, he is himself responsible for the general scheme.[2]

The Gospel as History. The Gospel falls into three sections :

1. The Ministry in Galilee (i. 14–ix. 50).
2. The last week in Jerusalem (xi. 1–xvi. 8).
3. These are separated by a brief and rather vague account of the period between them, x. 1–52 : i. 1–13 is introduction ; xvi. 9–20 is a later addition and not part of the original Gospel.

The story begins with the preaching of the Baptist, whose message of repentance is repeated by Jesus, Who proclaims that the Kingdom of God is at hand. Taking His stand with the apocalyptic hopes of His nation He wins the support of the people, but is quickly challenged by the religious

[1] *v.* R. H. Lightfoot, *History and Interpretation in the Gospels*, pp. 126 ff.
[2] An elaborate analysis of the sources of Mark is attempted by A. T. Cadoux in *The Sources of the Second Gospel*.

leaders. From iii. 6 to viii. 26 the Gospel is largely a series of stories without much chronological sequence, but the stories are not entirely disconnected. The reader is aware that despite His popularity there is a hardening of opposition, some hampering of His public words, and lack of freedom in His movements. At the end of the section He leaves Galilee, seeking seclusion in the north. It is a pause before the *dénouement*. He sees clearly that His own people will reject Him. At Caesarea Philippi is a climax when Peter, in the name of the rest, acknowledges Him as Messiah (viii. 27 ff.). The shadow of the Cross dominates the story from that point. He goes to Jerusalem to challenge the authorities by the Triumphal Entry and the Cleansing of the Temple. He is arrested and accused : first of blasphemy (" I will destroy this temple," xiv. 58), a charge which broke down ; and secondly of claiming to be Messiah, " Art thou the Christ, the Son of the Blessed ? " (xiv. 61, 62), to which His answer seems sufficient evidence to gain His condemnation. It may well be, at Lietzmann suggests, that " the result of a religious legal trial in the case of Jesus would have been by no means certain." [1] Therefore His Messianic claim is repre-

[1] *Der Prozess Jesu:* Sitzungsberichte der Königl. Preussischen Akademie der Wissenschaften : Jahrgang 1931, s. 321.

sented as a political charge and He is brought
before Pilate.   Mark describes His Messiahship as
hidden from all but a few throughout His ministry,
then acted in the Triumphal Entry, publicly acknowledged at His trial, and vindicated triumphantly by
the Resurrection.

Wrede[1] tried to prove that Mark composed his
Gospel out of the traditional material in accordance
not with the historical facts but with his own
theological ideas : no one ever thought Jesus was
Messiah in the days of His flesh, but Mark reads
it back into the earthly life, and so gives us an artificial arrangement, which may tell us much about
the faith of the Christian Church in the middle of
the century, but nothing that can be trusted about
the course of the Ministry, much less about the
inner consciousness of Jesus.   Wellhausen and
many others pressed home the attack in which the
formgeschichtliche school have proved vigorous
allies, since for them the whole framework of the
Gospel is nothing more than an " editorial construction."   But a more balanced judgment will conclude
that in the Gospel of Mark there is an account of
Jesus which does show how men came to believe
in Him, and why the Jews rejected Him, and their
leaders plotted and brought about His death, and

[1] *Das Messiasgeheimnis in den Evangelien.*

that the outline is " derived from the real memory
of real events " (F. C. Burkitt).[1] " Not every
incident in the Gospel must be taken as having
occurred precisely as described. Not every particular saying is a literal verbatim record. But the
Gospel narrative is in touch with reality and is the
outcome of genuine historical tradition. Some
such story is required as the historical explanation
of Christianity " (A. E. J. Rawlinson).

The Lost Ending. In the Codex Vaticanus and the
Codex Sinaiticus, in the Sinaitic Syriac and in some
ancient MSS. of the Ethiopic and Armenian Versions the Gospel ends at xvi. 8. All other MSS.
and Versions have the longer ending familiar in the
English Versions ; a few have in addition a shorter
ending which is not quoted by any early Greek or
Latin writers. One Old Latin MS. has this only.

The longer ending is in a different style from the
rest of the Gospel, and is clearly an epitome of the
appearances after the Resurrection, possibly, but
not probably, from a work of the Elder Aristion.[2]

J. Wellhausen, Johannes Weiss, E. Lohmeyer,
J. M. Creed, and B. H. Lightfoot are among those
who think xvi. 8 was the original end of the Gospel.

---

[1] *J.T.S.*, April 1935, p. 188.
[2] The last twelve verses are introduced by a rubric " of the Elder
Aristion " in an Armenian MS. of the tenth century.

Lightfoot maintains that so far as Markan usage is concerned xvi. 1–8 is satisfactory in form and complete. It was fitting for the Gospel to end " upon the note of trembling, fearfulness, and silence in the presence of the completed act of God in the work of man's salvation and its cost." [1] Other scholars are of opinion that unless the author for some reason left his work incomplete he would have gone on to relate the appearances of the Lord which were a part of the Church's tradition. Possibly, as Burkitt thought, he carried the story of the Gospel to cover the period dealt with in Acts i–xii. It may be that the original Gospel suffered mutilation, perhaps during the Neronian persecution. Streeter [2] thinks that the author of the Fourth Gospel derived the material in his last chapter from the lost ending of Mark, but this is only conjecture. It is likely that the original ending gave an account of an appearance to Peter and to the others in Galilee. It is certain that the copies of Mark which Matthew and Luke used ended at xvi. 8.

[1] *Locality and Doctrine in the Gospels*, p. 45.
[2] *The Four Gospels*, pp. 335 ff.

CHAPTER XIX

THE GOSPEL ACCORDING TO MATTHEW

Authorship and Original Language. There is a strong and consistent tradition in the early Church that the First Gospel was written by Matthew for Jewish Christians in their native tongue, Aramaic. Papias, Irenaeus,[1] Origen,[2] Eusebius,[3] and Jerome all agree in this, but it is possible that Papias [4] is the source from which the later writers derived their information; and he may be quoting John the Elder, as he is in his statement about the origin of Mark's Gospel. His words are Ματθαῖος μὲν οὖν Ἑβραΐδι διαλέκτῳ τὰ λόγια συνεγράψατο, ἡρμήνευσε δὲ αὐτὰ ὡς ἦν δυνατὸς ἕκαστος (so then Matthew composed the oracles in the Hebrew language, and each one interpreted them as he could). Few sentences in any early Christian writer have given rise to more controversy than this.

What is the meaning of τὰ λόγια (the oracles)? Eusebius and the others quoted seem to interpret the word as implying something in the nature of a Gospel. The word is used of the Old

---

[1] Eusebius, *Hist. Eccles.* v. 8.　　[2] *Ibid.*, vi. 25.
[3] *Ibid.*, iii. 24.　　[4] *Ibid.*, iii. 39.

Testament (Rom. iii. 2; Heb. v. 12). Clement of
Rome and Irenaeus use it in this sense. Therefore
F. C. Burkitt and many others interpret Papias's
words of a collection of Messianic proof-texts from
the Old Testament, a *Book of Testimonies*, which
Rendel Harris [1] thinks was one of the earliest
Christian books composed for the controversy
with the Jews. Streeter [2] maintains that it means
" oracular utterances," i.e. prophetic words of
Jesus mainly of an apocalyptic character. Papias
asserts that Matthew wrote these in Aramaic, and
that there was no authorized Greek translation. In
this Papias is quoting the Elder John, who, in defend-
ing the Fourth Gospel, Streeter suggests, is saying
that the Greek Gospel according to Matthew is not
to be regarded as an authoritative and accurate
representation of the original Aramaic.

1. There is a conflict of evidence. The tradition is strong that this Gospel was written in
Aramaic. But the internal evidence makes it certain that the Greek Gospel as it has come to us is
not a translation. For (*a*) the Greek is idiomatic
and flowing and in general free from Hebraisms;
(*b*) the Gospel is a compilation based on at least
two documents, one of which is Mark in Greek.

---

[1] *Testimonies*, Parts I and II.
[2] *The Four Gospels*, pp. 19 ff.

2. The Gospel is not by a personal follower of the Lord.

For (a) it makes use of earlier written documents, Mark, Q, and probably M ; (b) it shows a tendency to change or remove words or phrases in the primitive tradition which seemed to belittle the Lord and unduly to emphasize the obtuseness of the disciples ; e.g. Mark iii. 21, "For they said, He is beside himself" is not found in the parallel passage in Matthew; Mark x. 18, "Why callest thou Me good?" is in Matt. xix. 17 "Why askest thou Me about the good?" (cf. Mark i. 41, 43, and the omission of ὀργισθείς (D) and ἐμβριμησάμενος in Matt. viii. 3, 4); Mark iv. 13, "Do you not understand this parable, and how will you know all the parables?" is softened into, "Hear ye then the parable of the sower" (Matt. xiii. 18); Mark vi. 52, "For they did not understand about the loaves, but their heart was hardened," is replaced by Matt. xiv. 33, "They worshipped Him in the boat, saying, Truly Thou art God's son" (cf. the omission of Mark ix. 6a in Matthew's narrative of the Transfiguration).

3. The Gospel from the first was associated with the name of Matthew, the Apostle. Most likely this was because the important Church for which it was composed guaranteed it as an authentic record

of the Apostolic traditions according to Matthew.
If it is asked more definitely what was his connexion with the Gospel, no satisfactory answer can
be given. (*a*) It has been suggested that Matthew
was the author of an Aramaic gospel which was
early lost.   This was recognized as covering much
the same ground.   Jerome spoke of the " Gospel
according to the Hebrews," which he knew in
Aramaic as the original " Matthew." [1]   But enough
fragments of that Gospel have been discovered to
prove that it had no connexion with our First
Gospel, though it may have been a first-century
writing.   (*b*) More likely Matthew was the author
of one of the sources of the First Gospel ; either
of (1) a Book of Testimonies compiled out of
the Old Testament ; or (2) the peculiarly Matthaean
source which Streeter calls M ; but the writer of M
takes the Judaistic standpoint, not that of a tax-
collector (cf. xviii. 17) ; or (3) Q, a source which
consisted mainly of discourses, τὰ λόγια, if Streeter
is right in thus interpreting Papias.

Sources.   (*a*) In the discussion of the Synoptic
Problem the sources of this Gospel have been
analysed into Mark, Q, and M.   (*b*) The stories of
the Nativity have often been ascribed to a special
source which the Evangelist knew in a written form.

Vocatur a plerisque Matthaei authenticum.

But Streeter thinks that they belong to a cycle of tradition current in the Church for which this Gospel was written. To that cycle of narrative additions of this Gospel he assigns not only the first two chapters, but also the explanation of the Lord's Baptism (iii. 14 f.), the incident of Peter Walking on the Water (xiv. 28–31), the Stater in the Fish's Mouth (xvii. 24–27), and those stories connected with the Passion which are peculiar to Matthew's Gospel, the Price of the Treachery of Judas (xxvi. 14–16), and his Death (xxvii. 3–10), Pilate's wife's dream (xxvii. 19), and his Washing of his Hands (xxvii. 24 ff.), the Earthquake and Resurrection of the Saints (xxvii. 51–53), the Watch at the Tomb (xxvii. 62–66), the Rolling Away of the Stone at the Tomb (xxviii. 2–4), and the Bribery of the Guard (xxviii. 11–15). These are all distinguished by common stylistic features, by the emphasis on the fulfilment of prophecy and in the miraculous, and by the desire to justify the early traditions and to disarm criticisms of it.

(c) The author's interest in the fulfilment of prophecy is shown in the number of Old Testament quotations peculiar to himself, all introduced with " in order that that which was spoken by the prophets might be fulfilled," or similar words (i. 23, ii. 6, 15, 18, 23, iv. 15, 16, viii. 17, xii. 18–21,

xiii. 35, xxi. 5,[1] xxvii. 9–10).   All these, except
ii. 23, seem to be based upon the Hebrew,
whereas in the Old Testament quotations which
Matthew shares with the other Synoptic Gospels
the Septuagint is used.   The quotations which
are peculiar to this Gospel are comments upon
narrative ; those which are common to the other
Gospels are mostly in the words of Jesus.
Therefore it is thought that another of his sources
was a *Book of Testimonies*.   Tertullian and Cyprian
used such books which may well have been
based upon earlier collections of similar nature.
This might explain why he assigns to Jeremiah a
prophecy from Zechariah in xxvii. 9, 10, if he
was quoting from a section of the *Testimonies*
which began with a passage from Jeremiah.   The
objection is that some of these quotations, e.g.
ii. 15, 18, would not have much meaning in a
book of proof-texts apart from the narratives of the
Flight into Egypt and the Massacre of the Innocents.

Place of Origin.   If Streeter is right in thinking
that each of the four Gospels had the backing of an
influential Church, then his suggestion that this
Gospel was written for Antioch, though it cannot
be proved, has much to commend it.[2]   Antioch was

---

[1] This is also quoted in John xii. 15.
[2] *The Four Gospels*, pp. 500 ff.

an important Christian centre with a large Jewish population. This Gospel recognizes the universality of the Gospel, but yet has a marked Jewish undertone. If the author aims at reconciling the divergent parties, liberal and conservative, in the Church after the martyrdom of Paul and Peter and James for the same faith, as Streeter supposes, then the prominence given to Peter as the name round which all could rally would be appreciated in Antioch. Ignatius, Bishop of Antioch in the early part of the second century, seems to mean Matthew by "the Gospel," and he and the *Didache* bear witness to a type of Christianity in Antioch which in its Judaistic sympathy is akin to parts of Matthew.[1]

That the Gospel was written primarily for Jewish Christians is the tradition according to Irenaeus,[2] Origen,[3] and Eusebius,[4] and is supported by internal evidence. The portrait of the Messianic King, the emphasis on the fulfilment of prophecy, the interest in the attitude of Jesus to the Law, and the knowledge which the readers have of Jewish customs (cf. Matt. xv. 1 ff. with Mark vii. 1 ff.) are consistent with this destination. The translations

---

[1] Bacon's view is that this gospel arose in the Greek-speaking communities of Northern and North-eastern Syria. F. W. Green, in *The Gospel According to St. Matthew*, Clarendon Bible, suggests Edessa as the place of its origin.

[2] Eusebius, *Hist. Eccles.* v. 8.   [3] *Ibid.*, vi. 25.   [4] *Ibid.*, iii. 24.

of Hebrew words in i. 23, xxvii. 33, 46, and the explanation of the custom of releasing a prisoner at the Feast in Jerusalem (xxvii. 15) seem to show that the writer had other than Palestinian Jews in mind. Most likely, therefore, the Gospel was written for the Church in Antioch, or at any rate accepted as its Gospel by that Church.[1]

Date. (*a*) Since the author has used Mark and Q, the Gospel cannot be earlier than about A.D. 70, and since there is good evidence for its use in the Apostolic Fathers—Clement of Rome, the *Didache*, Ignatius, the *Shepherd* of Hermas, and Polycarp— it can hardly have been written later than A.D. 85–90. (*b*) That it was written after the fall of Jerusalem may be inferred from xxii. 7 and xxiii. 38. (*c*) This Gospel shows more interest in the apocalyptic hope than the others, stressing the immediacy of the visible Advent in the lifetime of those who had seen the Lord in the days of His flesh (x. 23, xxiv. 30). Streeter thinks that Matthew interprets the " abomination of desolation " (xxiv. 15) of the Anti-Christ in the light of the Nero-redivivus myth, which would have had special significance in Antioch, the eastern gate of the Roman Empire. Many would have suffered disappointment when

---

[1] According to the anti-Marcionite Prologue to Luke's Gospel, Matthew was written in Judæa. That may well be true of at least one of its sources.

the signs spoken of were fulfilled in the destruction of Jerusalem, and yet the expected " Consummation of the Age " tarried. Matthew may have written a few years after A.D. 70 to revive their waning hopes. (*d*) If it was intended as a Gospel of reconciliation between the parties who looked to James, Peter, and Paul as their leaders, then it is not likely to have been written until a decade or two after these chief Apostles had been martyred. (*e*) The allusions to the Christian *ecclesia* in xvi. 18, xviii. 17, and the tendency to minimize the shortcomings of the Twelve, suggest the latter part of the century.

On the whole, a date A.D. 80–85 seems most probable.

The Plan of the Gospel and the Aim of the Evangelist. There are two main divisions of the Gospel beginning, " From that time Jesus began . . ." (iv. 17 and xvi. 21). There is another introductory formula, " And it came to pass when Jesus ended . . .", which occurs five times (vii. 28, xi. 1, xiii. 53, xix. 1, xxvi. 1). Combining these two, we get this outline of the Gospel :

1. i. 1–iv. 16, Introductory : the Genealogy, Birth, Preparation for the Ministry, Baptism and Temptation.

2. iv. 17–xvi. 20. The Ministry in Galilee : the

growth of the disciples' faith in Jesus as Messiah, culminating in Peter's Confession. (*a*) iv. 17–vii. 27; (*b*) vii. 28–x. 42; (*c*) xi. 1–xiii. 52; (*d*) xiii. 53–xvi. 20.

3. xvi. 21–xxv. 46. (*a*) xvi. 21–xviii. 35, the end of the Ministry : in Galilee ; (*b*) xix. 1–xxv. 46 : the Journey to Jerusalem ; Discourses in Jerusalem.

4. xxvi. 1–xxviii. 20. The Passion and Resurrection.

The author's aim is revealed in this plan. He begins with the genealogy from Abraham, and traces the descent through the kingly line of David. He lays great stress on the title " Son of David,"[1] and on the royal dignity of the Lord. The Magi offer Him gifts for a king. Herod fears a rival to his throne. " The kingdom " occurs about twice as many times in this as in the other Synoptic Gospels. The priests point out that His birth fulfils the Old Testament prophecies. The Evangelist does not hesitate to re-arrange or even alter the material he has received, if it serves his purpose, which is to show what was the significance of Him Who appeared in the fulness of time, in whose life the words of Psalmists and Prophets

---

[1] Cf. i. 1, ix. 27, xii. 23, xv. 22, xx. 30, 31; xxi. 9, 15. In the other Gospels the title only occurs in the parallels to Matt. xx. 30, 31, and in our Lord's question to the Pharisees, Matt. xxii. 41 ff., etc.

found their fulfilment, Who was the Messiah of Whom Jewish history had been one long prophecy, Who came to fulfil the Old Law by making it New, Who was both King and Lawgiver of the new *ecclesia* which was the true people of God.

CHAPTER XX

THE GOSPEL ACCORDING TO LUKE AND THE ACTS OF THE APOSTLES

Authorship. There is almost universal agreement that the Third Gospel and Acts were the work of one author. The preface to the Gospel, Luke i. 1-4, is addressed to Theophilus, and Acts i. 1 is a secondary preface to the same patron, intended to recall the original, which was meant to cover both volumes. The style and vocabulary confirm the unity of authorship.

Until the last century there was universal agreement that the author was Luke. (1) Marcion, who had only this Gospel in his Canon, the Muratorian Fragment, Clement of Alexandria, etc., all attribute these writings to Luke, who hardly appears to have been so prominent that two volumes of such importance would have been assigned to him without due reason. (2) In the latter part of Acts there are four passages generally called " We " sections because the writer uses the first person plural (xvi. 10-17, from Troas to Philippi ; xx. 5-16, from Philippi to Miletus ; xxi. 1-18, from Miletus to Jerusalem ; xxvii. 1-xxviii. 16, the voyage from Caesarea to

Rome).[1] These appear to be notes from the diary of one of Paul's companions on his journeys. In vocabulary and style these sections are closely similar to the rest of the book, particularly to those chapters where he seems to be composing freely and not using written sources. The diary passages are among the most vivid in the book, and do not seem to have been edited. Therefore the argument that the author of the " We " sections is the author of Acts and also of the Gospel is strong, though Cadbury[2] attaches little importance to it. (3) The " diary " was written by one of Paul's companions on parts of the second and third journeys and on the voyage to Rome. If the evidence from the Captivity Epistles and 2 Timothy is admissible as to who were with Paul in Rome, Luke, Titus, Jesus Justus, and Crescens alone of these are not mentioned by name in Acts, or are not otherwise improbable. No one of the others can be regarded as having any claim to be the author, since universal tradition is in favour of Luke. That a friend of Paul wrote the Gospel and Acts is consistent with the general outlook of the author, as shown in his enthusiasm for the universality and freedom of the Gospel.

---

[1] Also xi. 28 in Codex Bezae (at Antioch).
[2] *The Style and Literary Method of Luke.*

(4) Hobart[1] and Harnack[2] maintained that the exact use of medical language in the Gospel and Acts confirmed the authorship of Luke, who in Col. iv. 14 is called a physician. But Cadbury[3] has shown conclusively that the vocabulary is not specially medical, that it is common to contemporary writers like Plutarch and Lucian, that is, to men of some culture and education. And from his very thorough sifting of the evidence Cadbury is confirmed in his view that the author is not " the beloved physician." But while it is clear that the evidence from the vocabulary does not prove the author was a physician, it is not inconsistent with it. As Cadbury himself admits, Hippocrates and Galen were accustomed to use the language of ordinary people. It may even be doubted whether there was a technical medical vocabulary in that age in the sense in which we understand it.

But many scholars do not believe that the author of the diary was the author of the rest of the book. Windisch,[4] for example, suggests that the author of Acts copied out passages from Luke's diary. But this is out of keeping with the way he has dealt with his sources Mark and Q in his first volume. Others

---

[1] *The Medical Language of St. Luke.*   [2] *Luke the Physician.*
[3] *The Style and Literary Method of Luke.*
[4] Foakes Jackson and Lake, *The Beginnings of Christianity*, vol. ii, pp. 298 ff.

attribute the diary to one hand, the narratives associated with the diary extracts to another, and suppose a final editor who used these sources and added Acts i–xv and the Gospel. But the evidence is not lightly to be set aside for believing that the author of the diary is identical with the compiler of Acts, and that means, for reasons already given, with the author of the Gospel. If the diarist was a friend and companion of Paul, then Luke is most probably its author. But the difficulty has been raised whether a companion of Paul could have written Acts, because it does not agree in important particulars with the letters of Paul.

(a) In his letters Paul is the champion of Gentile liberty who has proved in his own experience that salvation is by faith, not by the works of the Law: he is emancipated from Jewish practice. But in Acts he appears as loyal to the Law. He circumcised Timothy " because of the Jews," [1] though he tells the Galatians circumcision is nothing. He accepts the suggestion of the elders in Jerusalem to associate himself prominently with the purification of four men who were under a Nazirite vow in order to prove he is an orthodox Jew.[2] (But he tells the Corinthians, " To the Jews I became as a Jew, that I might gain Jews.") [3]

[1] xvi. 3.   [2] xxi. 21 ff.   [3] 1 Cor. ix. 20.

In Acts xv Paul accepts the compromise by which, though circumcision is not enforced, four[1] things which were displeasing to Jewish Christians were prohibited, although this is a denial of his principles, and seems to be a commendation of obedience to Jewish ordinances.   It is difficult to reconcile his attitude at the Council with his silence about the decrees in writing to the Galatians, especially if the visit to Jerusalem in Gal. ii. 1 ff. is the same as the visit in Acts xv. 2 ff.   (The difficulty is lessened if Galatians was written before the Council.   But it is more likely that the account in Acts xv of the Council is not strictly historical.   The author has confused an agreement, by which circumcision of the Gentiles was not to be obligatory, with another later council at which certain regulations were laid down to facilitate social intercourse between Jewish and Gentile members of the Church.)[2]

The speeches in Acts have little expression of the great doctrines which are so conspicuous in Paul's letters.   (But the diarist is unlikely to have been present to have heard the speeches, except that at Miletus,[3] and the address in Aramaic to the crowd at Jerusalem.[4]   They may be based on oral tradition, but hardly on written records.   But it is

---

[1] Three according to the Western text, omitting " things strangled."
[2] v. ch. iv, p. 54.   [3] xx. 18 ff.   [4] xxii. 3 ff.

scarcely possible for us to judge how far these speeches are the composition of the author of Acts following the familiar custom of ancient historians.)[1]

(b) In certain details of history, Acts and the Epistles are not in agreement. (i) The description of " Speaking with Tongues " on the Day of Pentecost makes it appear that the Apostles were speaking foreign languages.[2] In 1 Cor. xii the Gift of Tongues seems to mean the utterance of sounds, unintelligible to the hearers, although under the inspiration of the Spirit ; but there is no hint of ability to speak foreign languages. (Perhaps the author of Acts is rather interpreting the significance of the phenomenon, which seems to him to symbolize the universality of the Church.) (ii) The difficulty of reconciling the visits to Jerusalem mentioned in Acts ix. 26, xi. 30, and xv. 2 with the two visits in Gal. i. 18 and ii. 1 is considered in connexion with the Epistle to the Galatians.[3] (iii) There is some difficulty in reconciling the account of the movements of Paul's missionary companions between their departure from Thessalonica and their arrival in Corinth in Acts xvii. 16, xviii. 5, with Paul's words in 1 Thess. iii. 1, 6. And again in Acts ix. 24, " the Jews watched the gates (of Damascus) day

---

[1] v. Foakes Jackson and Lake, *The Beginnings of Christianity*, vol. v, pp. 402 ff.   [2] ii. 11.   [3] pp. 49 ff.

and night " is not in strict accord with 2 Cor.
xi. 32, "the ethnarch of Aretas was watching the
city to arrest me."

These and similar discrepancies throw some doubt
upon the tradition that a companion of Paul wrote
Acts ; but they prove only that the author of Acts
was writing without any knowledge of the Pauline
Epistles, and they make it almost impossible to
believe that Acts is a late compilation.   For anyone
writing in the second century would have been
careful to make his narrative agree in detail with the
authentic letters of the Apostle.   The arguments
already given for supposing that Luke was the
writer of the travel diary, and the author of the
whole book, and therefore also of the first volume,
the Gospel, are too strong to be set aside by these
divergencies.   If Luke wrote the " We " sections,
he was not present with Paul at all times or during
the greater part of his missionary activity ; he must
have depended on others for much of his information.   Luke is writing a history, Paul is concerned
with personal details.

Luke.   The only passages in which his name
occurs in the New Testament are Col. iv. 14, Philem.
24, 2 Tim. iv. 11.   The conjecture that he is to
be identified with Lucius of Cyrene,[1] one of the

---

[1] *v.* J. A. Findlay, *The Acts of the Apostles*, p. 47.

elders of the Church at Antioch (Acts xiii. 1), is partly based on the Western text of Acts xi. 28, which introduces another " We " section (" And there was great rejoicing, and when *we* were assembled "). It is less likely than that he was the " Man of Macedonia " whom Paul saw in his vision at Troas, as Ramsay supposes.[1] Perhaps he had been called in to attend Paul as a physician and had urged him to go to Europe, for he seems to join the Apostle at this point. " And when he had seen the vision, straightway *we* sought to go forth into Macedonia " (Acts xvi. 10). From the way the author of Acts describes Philippi, it may be presumed he was connected with it.[2] If Luke was the " Man of Macedonia," then he played a more important part in history than that of an historian. For the significance of Paul's crossing from Asia to Europe to preach the gospel was that he turned the course of civilization westwards.

Theophilus. It is impossible to do more than guess at the identity of the one to whom Luke dedicated his two volumes. The name may have been one given to him when he was received into the Church in baptism, a pseudonym designed to obscure his real name. The epithet in Luke i. 3, " Your

---

[1] *St. Paul, the Traveller and Roman Citizen*, pp. 202 ff.
[2] πρώτη τῆς μερίδος Μακεδονίας πόλις, κολωνία, xvi. 12.

Excellency," would be appropriate to a Roman official of equestrian or higher rank. Streeter conjectures further that Luke may have known this high-born Roman when he was governor of a province, perhaps Achaea, and that Luke wrote these two volumes to him after his return from his proconsulship as an *apologia* for Christianity to the Roman aristocracy. The further conjecture which Streeter ventures to make that Theophilus is none other than Flavius Clemens,[1] the heir to the throne, cannot of course be proved. The wife of Flavius Clemens, Domitilla, was a Christian, and her husband may have been an inquirer. If he were Theophilus, and if the malevolent suspicion of Domitian had not put him to death on a religious charge, he would have become the first Christian Emperor, and what that would have meant for the Church and for the world no one can calculate.

Date. It may be assumed that the two volumes were written consecutively. Three dates fall to be considered.

1. About A.D. 63. (*a*) Acts ends with Paul's imprisonment in Rome, where he is awaiting the issue of his appeal to Caesar. If the author knew what that issue was, would he not have completed the story with an account of Paul's acquittal, if he

---

[1] *The Four Gospels*, p. 535.

was acquitted; and of his subsequent re-arrest and martyrdom; or of Paul's and Peter's execution, and of the Fall of Jerusalem, if he had been writing after A.D. 70? Would there not be traces in his books of the bitterness left by the Neronian persecution? (*b*) If Luke knew that Paul visited Ephesus again, as the Pastoral Epistles are thought to imply, would he have left Paul's speech to the Ephesian Elders as it now stands with the prophecy falsified that they would not see his face again?[1] (*c*) If Paul visited Spain,[2] would it not have been mentioned as the fulfilment of the Lord's words in i. 8, if Acts was written later? (*d*) It is noted that the prophecy of Agabus (Acts xi. 28) was fulfilled; would it not have been noted that the prophecy of the destruction of Jerusalem in Luke xxi. 20 was fulfilled, if the author had been writing after A.D. 70? (*e*) The author of Acts shows no knowledge of the Pauline Epistles; probably, therefore, he wrote while he still had the personal companionship of the Apostle.[3]

But all these arguments are subjective, and even from the subjective point of view Luke might well have stopped where Acts stops, having worked out his theme, the expansion of the Church until Paul preached in Rome, the centre of the world. If he

[1] xx. 25, 38.   [2] Rom. xv. 24, 28.
[3] *v*, Harnack, *The Date of Acts and the Synoptic Gospels*.

is writing a defence of Christianity [1] to the Roman world, he might have thought it best to close his work before he needed to recount that his hero had been executed by that imperial power, which up to that time had protected the Christians against their enemies, the Jews.

The most serious objection to this early date is that it necessitates dating Mark, one of the sources of Luke's Gospel, as early as A.D. 50–60, which is possible, but very improbable.

2. About A.D. 100. The chief argument for this date is that Luke is thought to have read, or rather misread, the *Antiquities* of Josephus, which was not published until about A.D. 94. (*a*) in Luke iii. 1 (when) "Lysanias was tetrarch of Abilene." There was a Lysanias, to whom Josephus [2] refers, who was put to death by Antony in 34 B.C. Luke is thought to have made a blunder over that date. But an inscription makes it probable that there was a Lysanias ruling in Abilene in the reign of Tiberius. (*b*) In Acts v. 36, 37, Gamaliel is represented as speaking of two rebellions which came to nothing, one under Theudas, and " after this man rose up Judas of Galilee in the days of the enrolment." According to Josephus,[3] Theudas's rebellion was

---

[1] Streeter, *The Four Gospels*, p. 539 : " The Acts is really the first of the Apologies."

[2] *Ant.* xx. 7 ; cf. *Ant.* xix. 5. *Bell. Jud.* ii. 11. *v.* J. M. Creed, *The Gospel according to St. Luke*, pp. 307 ff.   [3] *Ant.* xx. 5.

N.T.—9*

in A.D. 44–45, ten years or more after Gamaliel was supposed to have been speaking; and Judas's rebellion was in A.D. 6–8. So there is a double anachronism. Josephus mentions these two together, but with no mistake in their relative dates. It is inferred that Luke had confused the dates through careless reading of Josephus. But there were many similar risings in the first half of the first century A.D., and Theudas is an abbreviation for several names, so that Luke may be referring to another and earlier rebellion of which nothing is known to us.[1] It seems unnecessary to attribute gross carelessness to a writer who, where it is possible to test him, is extraordinarily accurate. Therefore the supposed dependence of Luke on Josephus is not proved.

The books bear no traces of the Docetic controversy such as are found in the Fourth Gospel, which was probably written at the end of the century, and they contain many characteristics of an earlier date. If Luke was the author, he would have been hardly short of one hundred years old, but his writings show no signs of the decay of mental powers.

3. A.D. 75–85. (a) Luke xix. 43, xxi. 20, 24,

[1] Streeter, *The Four Gospels*, p. 557, suggests that possibly Luke may have heard Josephus lecture at Rome before the *Antiquities* was published, and his mistake was due to misreading of his notes.

suggest that the author has witnessed the fulfilment of prophecies about the destruction of Jerusalem. This is most clearly seen in the way Luke interprets the "abomination of desolation," in Mark xiii. 14, of the surrounding of Jerusalem by armies. (*b*) This date agrees with the most probable solution of the Synoptic problem, Luke's combination of QL with Mark. Some answer to the objection, why did not Luke describe Paul's martyrdom if he was writing after that had taken place, has been already offered.[1]

SOURCES

1. *The Gospel.* The Third Gospel falls into five main sections :

(*a*) i.–ii.   The Birth and Infancy of the Baptist and of Jesus.

(*b*) iii. 1–iv. 13.   The Mission of the Baptist; the Baptism and Temptation of Jesus.

(*c*) iv. 14–ix. 50.   The Ministry in Galilee.

(*d*) ix. 51–xix. 28.   The Journey to Jerusalem.

(*e*) xix. 29–xxiv. 53.   The Last Days at Jerusalem ; the Passion and Resurrection.

[1] The anti-Marcionite Prologue to the Gospel of Luke says he " was of Antioch in Syria, by profession a physician, who, having been a disciple of the Apostles and afterwards having followed Paul until his martyrdom, and having served the Lord continuously, without wife and without children, fell asleep at the age of 84 years in Boeotia, being full of the Holy Ghost." The Prologue also states that Luke wrote his Gospel in Achaea after the Gospels of Mark and Matthew had been written.

The whole of (*a*) and much of (*d*) is peculiar to Luke. "The great Interpolation" is a name that used to be assigned to (*d*) on the theory that Mark was the framework of the Gospel. The name is a misnomer according to the Proto-Luke hypothesis.

From Luke i. 1–4 it may be inferred that Luke was not an eye-witness, but that he had conversed with eye-witnesses of the events he records; that he had used the written records which others had made before him; that he had carefully investigated his sources and aimed at writing chronologically.

(*a*) Among the "many who had taken in hand to draw up a narrative concerning those matters which have been fulfilled among us" are Mark and Q.

(*b*) If the Proto-Luke hypothesis is right, he had himself composed a first draft of his Gospel by combining Q with L.

(*c*) He added large sections of Mark to this first draft.

(*d*) The Infancy Narratives (ch. i. 5–ii) are from a special source. The Prologue (i. 1–4) is in polished literary Greek, the rest of the first two chapters is in the archaic style of the Septuagint. C. C. Torrey[1] is of opinion (and many modern scholars) that these chapters were originally in

---

[1] *The Composition and Date of Acts.*

Hebrew, or at any rate the hymns in them, the Magnificat, the Benedictus, and the Nunc Dimittis, since Hebraisms abound in them. Since Luke shows no signs elsewhere of knowing Hebrew, it is presumed that he used them in a Greek translation, retouching them in his own style.[1] But the agreement of the style with that of Luke himself is such that many scholars believe the chapters are an example of Luke's literary art, by which he has composed these stories in the style of the Septuagint in accordance with the primitive Jewish-Christian tradition and spirit. It seems probable that the material for the Infancy Stories was not known to Luke when he put together Proto-Luke, but that he prefixed them to his finished work when he combined Proto-Luke with Mark.

2. *Acts.* The book falls into two nearly equal parts :

(1) i. 1–xv. 35, the Acts of the Spirit in the Church culminating in the admission of the Gentiles in ch. xv. The tone of this part is historical.

(2) xv. 36–xxviii. 31, the expansion of the Church

---

v. W. F. Howard on " Semitisms in the New Testament " in Moulton and Howard's *Grammar of New Testament Greek*, vol. ii, pp. 482–483 : " The Hebraic phraseology is beyond question, but there is nothing that lies beyond the range of composition by one who was steeped in the diction of the Greek version of the Psalter."

until it reaches Rome; the hero of this part is Paul, and the tone is biographical.

(1) Since Luke i. 1–4 is a preface to the whole work, it may be inferred that Luke's sources were in volume II, as in volume I, eye-witnesses and written records. Since "all narratives, of course, are ultimately traceable to the places where the actors lived and moved" (McNeile),[1] it would be expected that the narratives in this section would have emanated from Jerusalem, Antioch, and Caesarea. This is the more likely, since among the sources of the Gospel are Q (Antiochene) and L (Caesarean).

Harnack thought there was a Jerusalem source A (iii. 1–iv. 31), and parallel to it, but not so trustworthy, a Jerusalem source B (i, ii, v. 17–42). Lake [2] thinks this source B may be a continuation of the Jerusalem source used by Luke in his narrative of the Passion and Resurrection. In xv. 1–35 is also found the tradition preserved by the Jerusalem Church.

(b) The Caesarean tradition in Lake's view is behind viii. 26–40, ix. 31–x. 48. Other passages in this section may be a combination of a Jerusalem with a Caesarean source.

---

[1] *Introduction to the New Testament*, p. 82.
[2] *The Beginnings of Christianity*, ii. pp. 145 ff.

(c) A third source is probably connected with Antioch—ix. 1–30, xi. 19–30, xii. 24–xiv. 28. This source may overlap with the Jerusalem source, and if so, the serious problem of identifying Paul's visits to Jerusalem in Acts and Galatians can be solved if the famine visit in Acts xi. 30 is a duplicate of the Council visit in Acts xv, the one from the Antiochene and the other from the Jerusalem source —and both are identical with the second visit in Gal. ii.

If it is right to analyse the first half of Acts into these sources, they have doubtless received editorial redaction and additions from the author of the whole book. F. Blass some years ago suggested that there was one source emanating from Jerusalem, due to Mark, a continuation of his Gospel, which ended at xvi. 8, carrying the story of the early Church up to Acts xv. 35, and Luke used it as he has used Mark's Gospel.

C. C. Torrey[1] supposes a single Aramaic document came from a Judæan Christian who was specially interested in the admission of the Gentiles to the Church and who considered that the decrees of Acts xv settled the question. The author of Acts has translated it verbatim, having first seen it when he arrived in Rome, A.D. 62.

---

[1] *The Composition and Date of Acts.*

Later he added a second part to his book, and thus made a sequel to his Gospel which was already written. It seems most improbable that the first part of Acts has one source only, but that the sources, whether written or oral, were originally in Aramaic is what would be expected, and that they were local traditions connected more or less closely with individuals is a reasonable hypothesis.

(2) The source of the second half of Acts is less hypothetical. Luke has used his own diary for the " We " sections ; and he may well have been present at other times when he does not use the first person plural, e.g. during Paul's stay in Jerusalem at his arrest, and when he was held a prisoner at Caesarea (xxi. 18–xxvi. 32). He may at least have been near enough to have accurate knowledge, even if he was not himself always an eye-witness. Paul himself and Paul's friends could have been other sources of information on which he could draw.

The Western Text. Some of the most striking differences between the Western and Neutral texts occur in Luke-Acts, especially in the latter. The Western text inserts the story of the Man Working on the Sabbath in place of Luke vi. 5, but on the whole is shorter than the Neutral and is specially noteworthy for some omissions in the last three chapters of the Gospel which Hort called Western non-interpolations.[1] But in Acts the Western text is longer and often more vivid. Blass thought that Luke wrote two editions of both books—the Neutral text represents the first edition of the Gospel and the second of Acts. But most scholars think the decision, so far as Acts is concerned, must be between accepting the longer (Western) version as original and the shorter as a scholarly revision of it later—a view which has been defended with much learning recently by A. C. Clark [2]—or accepting the shorter (Neutral) text as original, and the other as due to editorial additions and paraphrases.[3] It is probable that the additions of the Western text are in many cases accurate, though they may not be original.

Characteristics of the Gospel. Luke planned a more ambitious work than either of the other Evangelists and was well equipped for his task.

1. He shows considerable command of the Greek language and can vary his style with great effect. Though it is probable he knew neither Hebrew nor Aramaic, he could write in excellent imitation of the translation Greek of the Septuagint. Or, again,

---

[1] Luke xxii. 19b, 20, xxiv. 12, 36, 40, 51b.

[2] *The Acts of the Apostles.*

[3] This is the view of J. H. Ropes in *The Beginnings of Christianity*, vol. iii.

he can draw graphic pen portraits, e.g. of Zacharias and Zacchaeus, in the Greek natural to the cultured Hellenist of his day. Renan rightly says this " is the most literary of the Gospels." The narrative is constructed on a large scale, and the author can tell a story with both pathos and restraint.

2. This Gospel attempts a more complete picture of the Lord, the preparation for His coming in the birth of the Forerunner, the Infancy, Boyhood, and Ministry. That Jesus was more than the Messiah of Jewish nationalism is clear in all the Gospels, but Luke especially emphasizes the note of universalism.

3. In Mark Jesus is an austere, mysterious figure; in Matthew the giver of the new Law; in Luke He is seen in social intercourse with men and women, revealing in His own attitude to Samaritans, women, sinners, and publicans, the true meaning of the brotherhood of man and the Fatherhood of God. Many of the most striking parables and sayings in this Gospel are concerned with wealth and poverty and social relationships.

4. Prayer, praise and thanksgiving, and the Holy Spirit have a prominent place in the Gospel, in connexion with the example of Jesus and direct instruction of the disciples. The first scene and the last are of worship in the Temple.

5. Luke shows a special interest in angels and the miraculous. That does not mean that he deliberately emphasizes the supernatural in the interests of dogma rather than of truth, but that for him there was no hard-and-fast line between the natural and the supernatural. There was no doubt in his mind that Christianity was miraculous.

All these traits in the Gospel can be equally illustrated by the narratives of Acts, in which there is rather less restraint in regard to the supernatural. But there may be nothing contrary to experience in the atmosphere of mingled fear and wonder and power in which the believers lived.

Luke's Aim in Acts. In i. 8, " But ye shall receive power, when the Holy Ghost is come upon you : and ye shall be my witnesses both in Jerusalem, and in all Judæa and Samaria, and unto the uttermost part of the earth," he states a double thought on which his book is based : (1) the power possessed by the Apostles through the Holy Spirit, which was a proof of their divine commission ; (2) the gradual expansion of the Church partly in numbers, through this power of the Apostles, partly in geographical extent. These are two sides of one truth : in the Gospel Luke tells Theophilus he related " all that Jesus began to do and to teach until His Ascension "—and since Jesus is still man, His Incarnation is embodied in the Church—so that when Jesus had begun His work on earth, He continued it in the Church. This is shown by the parallel between the history of Jesus in the Gospel and the history of the two chief Apostles in Acts : (1) an introductory period of waiting and preparation (Luke i. ii of Jesus ; Acts i of Peter ; ix. 30, xi. 25, 26 of Paul). (2) The gift of the Spirit consecrating to their ministry (Luke iii. 21, 22 ; Acts ii. 1–11, xiii. 2, 3). (3) A period of public ministry, preaching, healings : the rise of opposition (Luke iv.–xxi ; Acts ii. 14–xi, xiii. 4–xxi. 26). (4) A period of suffering (Luke xxii.–xxiii ; Acts xii. 1–6, xxi. 27–xxviii. 16). (5) Deliverance in preparation for further activity (Luke xxiv ; Acts xii. 7–19, xxviii. 17–31). The great events which he had recounted in the Gospel as having been begun in Galilee were only a beginning. The power which possessed the disciples after Pentecost was from their Master ; it was the common possession of them all and could be so taken for granted that they did not hesitate to say, " It seemed good to the Holy Spirit and to us." [1] The Acts is not inaptly called the " Gospel of the Holy Spirit."

The Historical Value of Acts. It must be admitted regretfully that the book is incomplete from

---

[1] xv. 28.

the point of view of history. Many details are omitted which would be of great value to us in studying the growth of the early Church. We are curious to know more of the Church in Rome. When was it founded, by whom? So of the Churches in Alexandria and in Babylon. What was the constitution and worship of the Church of earliest days? But Luke was not a mere collector of stories like the fabricators of the many books of Acts of one or other of the Apostles of a later date.[1] He was no mere collector of antiquities : he was an historian, though not according to modern standards. He had a fixed aim and has planned his book with care. So he has only space for single scenes, often very vivid in detail, which must in nearly every case have been typical of many others. For example, he pictures preaching in the outer court of the Temple (chs. ii and iii); the attitude of Christians before Jewish tribunals (chs. iv and v); the working of signs—the lame man in the Temple, the healing of Aeneas and Dorcas—the lame man at Lystra (chs. iii, ix, xiv); the election and organization of church officers (ch. vi); a Christian martyr (ch. vii); a confirmation (ch. viii); a proconsul's court (at Paphos in Cyprus) (ch. xiii); a Sabbath Service in a Synagogue (at Antioch) (ch. xiii); a

[1] M. R. James, *The Apocryphal New Testament*.

Christian Council (ch. xv); a riot (ch. xix); a sermon to Jews (at Antioch) (ch. xiii), to ignorant pagans (at Lystra) (ch. xiv), to philosophers (at Athens) (ch. xvii); a defence of Christianity in a Roman court (ch. xxiv); a voyage and shipwreck (ch. xxvii).

It is noteworthy that Luke does not set up a single personality, not even Paul, as the central point : no other personality but Christ could be the centre. He has a strong sense of historical development, and generally speaking is correct in his observation and information. He is familiar with the difference between senatorial and imperial provinces. Cyprus is a senatorial province under a proconsul.[1] He knows the local name of magistrates at Thessalonica—politarchs.[2] Ramsay, who went out to excavate in Asia Minor convinced that Acts was a second-century document of little value, has been so impressed by facts like these that he has been won to declare it a first-century document by Luke, and an historical record of the first quality.

The book is honest—it gives no fancy picture of the Church in its golden age ; there are unworthy elements in it, such as Ananias and Sapphira. The fervent communism of the early days is hardly a

[1] xiii. 7.　　　[2] xvii. 8.

success, and seems to have produced a Church which was dependent on the charity of others.

The author has his limitations : in chronology his work is defective—and since he is dependent on others for much of his information, he does not tell us, perhaps because he does not know, much that we should like to know, e.g. about Paul's three years in Ephesus—was he imprisoned there, and why, and how was he released ?   Luke belonged to an age which accepted signs and wonders without criticism, which saw divine control directly at work in events.   A Christian historian of to-day would trace the human influences at work between the event and the ultimate cause in the will of God. Luke in short is more interested in and less critical of the miraculous than we are.

Again in comparison with Paul's letters, as has already been shown, there are divergencies ; but it can hardly be right to paint the portrait of Paul only out of the colours we find in his own letters. We have only a part of his correspondence.   Luke may make little of the length and strength of the opposition of the Jewish Christians in Jerusalem to the admission of the Gentiles into the Church except on their terms.   From Paul's Epistles it is clear that the controversy was carried on for years. Luke may give a not quite correct impression of the

Council at Jerusalem in Acts xv. He stresses the unity of the Church, whereas Paul is concerned with the personal question in his letters.

Behind the differences there is to be set the substantial agreement of the letters of Paul and the Book of Acts, which in many remarkable ways confirm and supplement each other. Harnack was justified in saying, " Direct touch with the recorded facts alone explains such a history as lies before us in the Acts of the Apostles."

In answer to the criticism that the book ends disappointingly, Streeter compares the concluding words to Greek tragedy, which ends " with words of good omen on a note of calm." [1] The author has traced the growth of the Christian Church in power and geographical extent ; he brings the narrative to the point where the greatest missionary of the new religion has come to the capital of the empire, and although he is a prisoner he has a large measure of freedom, which is what Luke emphasizes. He has told how the Jews murdered Jesus, the Jews persecuted His followers, but among the last words of his book are, " Behold we go to the Gentiles—they will hear." Theophilus would understand and appreciate the significance of that prophecy.

[1] *The Four Gospels*, p. 539.

PART VI

THE JOHANNINE WRITINGS

CHAPTER XXI

THE FOURTH GOSPEL

Authorship. The author is identified with the
" disciple whom Jesus loved " in John xxi. 24 :
" This is the disciple which witnesseth of these
things and wrote these things ; and we know that
his witness is true." The reasons for thinking " the
disciple whom Jesus loved " was John the son of
Zebedee may be briefly summarized thus :

1. The tradition which supports it is as old as
the second century. Papias speaks of two Johns :
the Apostle and the Elder.[1] Irenaeus calls Papias a
" hearer of John," i.e. of the Apostle. Irenaeus
had as a boy, he says,[2] heard Polycarp, a disciple of
John, the son of Zebedee, and Irenaeus connects
that John with Ephesus,[3] and calls him the " Beloved Disciple " and attributes to him the Gospel,
the Apocalypse, and 1 and 2 John. Clement of
Alexandria cites the Apostle John as the author
of the Gospel, and so do Tertullian and
Origen. According to tradition, John the Apostle

---

[1] Eusebius, *Hist. Eccles.*, iii. 39.
[2] *Ibid.*, v. 20.
[3] Iren. *Adv. Haer*, iii. 1.

lived to extreme old age in Ephesus (cf. John xxi. 23).[1]

2. In the Synoptic Gospels John the son of Zebedee is one of the intimate circle which includes Peter and James. In Acts and the Pauline Epistles he is prominent as a pillar of the Church. In the Fourth Gospel John, the disciple, is not mentioned by name. It would be strange if he were not mentioned at all. Of the two who were the Baptist's disciples and " who followed Jesus " in John i. 35, Andrew is identified, not the other. An unnamed disciple is associated with Peter at the trial (xviii. 15). The " Beloved Disciple " is associated with Peter at the Last Supper, at the Empty Tomb, and at the Appearance beside the Lake, where the group of disciples includes the sons of Zebedee.

But there is another tradition which asserts that John the son of Zebedee was martyred early. The evidence for this is :

1. In a seventh or eighth-century Epitome of the History of Philip of Side (fifth century) it is written " Papias in his second book says that John the divine (δ $\theta\epsilon o\lambda \acute{o}\gamma o\varsigma$) and James his brother were slain by the Jews." Georgius Hamartolus (ninth century) is claimed to support this, but is more

---

[1] An excellent summary of the external evidence on the whole question is given by W. F. Howard in *The Fourth Gospel in Recent Criticism and Interpretation*, pp. 247–251.

likely to be merely repeating it, when he says that both the sons of Zebedee met with a violent death in fulfilment of the Lord's words in Mark x. 39. Though many scholars have accepted this as authentic, J. H. Bernard has presented a strong case against it and concludes, "no historical inference can be drawn from a corrupt sentence in a late epitome of the work of a careless and blundering historian"[1]

2. According to some Syriac martyrologies, John and James are commemorated on the same day. But these belong to a time[2] when all the Apostles were credited with martyrdom, and they are not of much value as evidence.

3. The promise to the sons of Zebedee that they should be baptized with the baptism with which the Lord was baptized is interpreted as a prophecy that both James and John would suffer martyrdom, and it is suggested it was attributed to the Lord *post eventum*. But there is no need to doubt the historicity of the story. Baptism was in the later Church a synonym for martyrdom; but in the context it could well be a prediction of pain and suffering, not of death, in the cause of Christ. It may be that the word of Christ gave rise to the tradition.

4. No early Christian writer before Irenaeus re-

---

[1] *Commentary on St. John*, vol. i, p. xlii. [2] A.D. 411.

fers to the residence of John in Asia Minor.[1] This is a serious difficulty, but the argument from silence is not conclusive.

Together with the tradition that John the Apostle was the author of the Gospel, there are hints that others were associated with him in writing it. In the Gospel itself (xxi. 24) others set their seal to the truth of what is written ; and in xix. 35 the writer seems distinguished from the witness. In the Muratorian Fragment it is said, " The disciples fasted and prayed, and it was revealed to Andrew that John should describe all things in his own name ; for he professes he was a spectator and hearer and writer of all the wonders of the Lord in order." Irenaeus has the unusual word " John *gave out* the Gospel in Ephesus " (ἐξέδωκε τὸ εὐαγγέλιον ἐν Ἐφέσῳ).[2]

That the author of the Gospel is the author of the Johannine Epistles is supported by early tradition, by the likeness of the theological ideas in the Gospel and 1 John, and by the similarity in style and diction between the Gospel and the three Epistles.[3] The writer of 2 and 3 John calls

---

[1] *v.* R. H. Charles, *Commentary on Revelation*, vol. i, p. xlv.

[2] Iren. *Adv. Haer*, iii. 1.

[3] *v.* W. F. Howard, *The Fourth Gospel in Recent Criticism and Interpretation*, in an appendix on "The Linguistic Unity of the Gospel and Epistles," pp. 252 ff.

himself the Elder. Therefore the writer of the Gospel was the Elder. This is confirmed by 1 John i. 1–3. John the Elder was a disciple of the Lord according to Papias, although not one of the Twelve.

It is possible to reconcile the divergencies in the evidence by assuming that the Evangelist is the Elder, but the Witness who is the authority behind the Gospel is John the Apostle. " This is the disciple which . . . wrote these things " (xxi. 24) is the testimony of those who thus guaranteed that the Gospel had apostolic authority behind it, and was added by those who published the Gospel; or " wrote " may be understood, as Bernard suggests, in the sense " caused to be written," though not in the sense of dictated. The relation between the two may be compared to that of Mark in his Gospel with Peter.

(a) This solution does justice to the tradition of apostolic authorship and to the tradition that the Apostle was not alone in writing it. (b) It accounts for the fact that some Christians [1] rejected this Gospel despite its apostolicity. (c) The Gospel shows familiarity with the topography of Jerusalem [2] and Palestine, [3] with Jewish doctrine and Rabbinic

---

[1] The Alogi.
[3] iv. 6, vi. 1, xi. 54.
[2] v. 2, xi. 18, xix. 13.

methods of argument.[1] The writer stresses the Messiahship, but along with this Jewish idea he introduces the philosophic conception of the Logos. The Apostle was a Jew, the Elder may have been. To the former the intimate knowledge of Jewish customs is due, to the latter the philosophic background, "the interpretative transformations," may be attributed. So that this solution meets the difficulty that a Galilean fisherman was not likely to have attained the intellectual development of the writer of such a Gospel. (d) The writer of the Gospel has made use of Mark and Luke. An Apostle would hardly have done this, but one writing with apostolic authority behind him might well have corrected these earlier Evangelists, which is what the author of this Gospel appears to do.

The majority of English scholars incline to the belief that the authority of the Apostle John is behind this Gospel, though opinions differ widely as to how much is to be attributed to the Apostle and how much to the Evangelist. Continental scholars for the most part attach little or no importance to the tradition that associates John the son of Zebedee with Ephesus or with any of the "Johannine" writings.

If the Evangelist is the Elder mentioned in 2

[1] Cf. the argument in chs. v, vii, viii, ix.

and 3 John, there is some reason to identify him, as Streeter and many other scholars, with the Elder John whom Papias described as one of the disciples of the Lord. Streeter thinks that this " Elder's rather critical words about Mark's and Matthew's Gospels [1] are a defence of his own Gospel which was attacked because it was in some points at variance with the others. The identification cannot be proved, but we know of no other who was called ' the Elder.' "

Ingenious attempts have been made to identify the " Beloved Disciple " with Lazarus, John Mark, the Rich Young Ruler, an influential citizen of Jerusalem, whose knowledge of Jesus was confined to the Jerusalem Ministry, and who was not one of the Twelve. But these take no account of the tradition which connects the son of Zebedee with the Gospel. The conjecture that the " Beloved Disciple " is an ideal figure who represents the superiority of those " who have not seen and yet have believed " is not borne out by the evidence of the Gospel. It may be, as Streeter suggests, that John the son of Zebedee is idealized as the " Beloved Disciple." The title was given him by the Evangelist. But Streeter accepts the tradition that he was martyred, perhaps in the Jewish War, A.D.

---

[1] Eusebius, *Hist. Eccles.*, iii. 39.

68. If that were so, how did the tradition arise of his tarrying until the Lord came, to which the Gospel itself bears witness ?[1] That tradition was known in Ephesus, where the Gospel arose, and Streeter's explanation of confusion between John the Apostle, John the Elder, and John the Seer is not altogether satisfactory.

Relation of the Fourth to the Synoptic Gospels. (*a*) From the Synoptic Gospels it would be assumed that the Ministry lasted about one year. In the Fourth Gospel there is a definite scheme of chronology. The call of the disciples seems to have taken place in the early spring (i. 19–ii. 11), sometime before Jesus goes to the First Passover (ii. 13). After a period in Jerusalem, then in the land of Judæa (i.e. outside Jerusalem), He goes through Samaria to Galilee, and (if, as seems likely, ch. vi should be transposed before ch. v) feeds the multitude at the time of the Second Passover (vi. 4). He then goes up to Jerusalem for the Feast of Pentecost (v. 1). Because the Jews sought to kill Him, He went again to Galilee, and later in the autumn went up to the Feast of Tabernacles (vii. 2). He was in Jerusalem in the winter following at the Feast of Dedication (x. 22). He went away beyond Jordan, and then to Bethany, near Jerusalem. After

[1] xxi. 23.

the Raising of Lazarus He went to a city called
Ephraim, and six days before the Third Passover
He came again to Bethany (xii. 1), and just before
the Feast was arrested and crucified.

(b) From this chronological outline it is clear
that the greater part of the Ministry in John is in
and around Jerusalem, whereas in the Synoptic
Gospels Jesus does not come to Jerusalem until
the last week. But there are hints even in the earlier
Gospels of visits to Jerusalem, e.g. the story of the
Temptation. It is difficult to suppose that all the
material in Luke ix. 51–xix. 27 is to be fitted into
the one journey from Galilee to Jerusalem. There
is the lament over Jerusalem—" *how often* would I
have gathered," etc. (Matt. xxiii. 37). The only
Galilean teaching in John is in vi. 26 ff.

(c) There are many differences of historical detail.
The Baptist's Ministry according to the earlier Gospels is ended before Christ's Ministry begins. In
John they overlap. The Cleansing of the Temple
is at the end in the Synoptic Gospels, where it is
the immediate cause of the arrest. In John it is at
the beginning, and the Raising of Lazarus takes its
place as that which causes the authorities to resolve
on action against Jesus forthwith.[1] According to

---

[1] For the significance of this *v.* W. F. Howard, *The Fourth Gospel in
Recent Criticism and Interpretation*, pp. 155–157.

the Synoptic narrative the Last Supper is the Passover Meal, but according to John it takes place
the night before, and Jesus is crucified at the time
when the Passover Lamb was being killed. There
are, however, traces of inconsistency in the Synoptic
account (cf. Mark xiv. 1, 2, xv. 21, 46 ; Luke xxii.
15–16). Although the selection of events in the
Fourth Gospel is so different from that of the first
three Gospels, it may be that some incidents which
are not at first sight parallel are to be connected.
Nicodemus (John iii) is thought to be another version of the Rich Young Ruler (Mark x. 17 ff.) ;
the Paralytic at Bethesda (John v) identical with the
Paralytic at Capernaum (Mark ii) ; the Man born
Blind (John ix) with Bartimaeus (Mark x). But
the identification of these and similar incidents
involves as many difficulties as it tries to solve.

(d) In the style of the discourses there is a striking
difference between the Fourth and the other Gospels.
There are no parables in the Synoptic sense in John.
It is difficult to find the break where the Johannine
Christ ends and the Evangelist's interpretation
begins. Streeter describes the discourses in John
as " interpretative transformations," and calls attention to the fact that the Synoptic Gospels seem to
reflect Jewish practice of preserving *ipsissima verba*,
while John's is more akin to the Greek practice of

putting into the mouth of historical characters speeches of the historian's own composition. But the Johannine and the Synoptic Christ speak with the same tone of authority—aphoristic sayings are common to both; and in Matt. xi. 25 ff. it is clear that according to the Synoptic witness Jesus spoke at times in the Johannine style. Jewish writers support the authenticity of the discourses in John.[1]

(e) The portraits of Christ in the Synoptic Gospels represent Him with a different emphasis in each case, but they have more in common with each other than either has with the Johannine Christ, Who in the Prologue is identified with the Logos, Who is recognized as the Messiah from the first.

(f) In John there is no account of the Virgin Birth, the Baptism, the Temptation, the Transfiguration, the Institution of the Supper, the Agony in Gethsemane, the Ascension. But although the Fourth Gospel discards some elements in the Synoptic tradition, it sometimes conserves them in a different form.[2]

It has been generally agreed that John knew Mark, for in his Gospel are found some of the peculiar phrases of Mark, e.g. John vi. 7 (Mark

---

[1] For an examination of the Johannine sayings of Jesus v. W. F. Howard, *The Expository Times*, vol. xlvi, no. 11, pp. 486–491.

[2] E.g. The Agony in the Garden, cf. xii 27.

vi. 57), John xii. 3, 5 (Mark xiv. 3, 5).   C. H. Dodd
suggests that John vi. 1–vii. 10 is dependent on the
order of events in Mark vi. 31–x. 1.   Certainly of
the few sayings in the Fourth Gospel, which are at
all like those in the Synoptic Gospels, all but one
(John xiii. 16) are found in Mark.

The probability that John knew Luke is derived
from the names Martha and Mary (John xii. 5 ;
Luke x. 38), and from the fact that both place the
first Resurrection Appearance in Jerusalem, and
not in Galilee (as Mark probably).   But Gardner-
Smith,[1] re-examining the evidence in detail, has
thrown doubt upon the knowledge by John of the
Synoptic Gospels.   He claims that the Fourth
Gospel is independent of the others.

Is the Gospel Composite ?   (*a*) Ch. xxi is clearly an
appendix, for the Gospel ends at xx. 31.   There is
an awkwardness about the failure of the disciples
to recognize the Risen Lord after xx. 24, and about
the sudden change of locality to Galilee.   In regard
to the Parousia, xxi. 22 is hardly in agreement with
xiv. 2, 3, 18, 19.   But though the chapter is an
appendix, there is no reason to believe it was added
in the middle of the second century to commend
the Gospel to the Church in Rome, as Holtzmann
and Bacon thought.   The Gospel was never known

[1] *Saint John and the Synoptic Gospels.*

without this appendix, and the argument from style and language is such that there need be little doubt it was written by the author of chs. i-xx. He seems to have added it to correct some misunderstanding about a word of Jesus concerning Peter and the Beloved Disciple and the Parousia.

(b) Many attempts have been made to analyse the Gospel into sources composed of *logia* and a framework of narrative (Wendt), or a foundation document much like the Marcan outline (Wellhausen), and so on. More recently Burney claimed that there was an Aramaic Gospel written about A.D. 75-80, that this was translated into Greek, and was substantially the Fourth Gospel. Torrey[1] has made this claim about all the Gospels, but he and Burney do not always agree upon the mistranslations of the Aramaic. It may be that the Evangelist thought in Aramaic, but if so be translated his thought so that he composed his Gospel in Greek. Certainly the connexion between discourses and narratives is too intricate to give ground for partition theories. The unity of the book is such as is due to an author, not to an editor; although there are probably a few verses which are of the nature of glosses (e.g. iv. 1, 2).

Misplacements. Since, from the *Fragments of an*

---

[1] *The Four Gospels, a new translation.*

Unknown Gospel[1] recently acquired by the British Museum, it is known that the papyrus codex as distinguished from the papyrus roll was in use as early as the first half of the second century for Christian writings, the hypothesis that in early copies of books of the New Testament papyrus sheets may have become disarranged is reasonable, and most scholars are agreed that in the Fourth Gospel it is probable. There are two re-arrangements which are widely accepted.

1. In iv. 54 Jesus is at Cana ; in v. 1 He goes to Jerusalem to a feast unnamed ; in vi. 1 He crosses the Lake to Capernaum. If vi. 1 follows iv. 54, He does not go to Jerusalem, until after the Feeding of the Multitude. Perhaps also the denunciation of the Jews in v. 44–47 was originally followed by vii. 15–24. Then vii. 1–14 and vii. 25 ff. follow naturally.

2. In xiv. 30 it is written, "I will no more speak much with you," and in xiv. 31, "Arise, let us go hence." Then follow three chapters of discourse. The simplest change is to transpose xiv. 25–31 to the end of ch. xvi (Streeter). Another suggestion is that originally chs. xv and xvi stood between xiii. 31a and xiii. 31b. Bernard's re-arrangement is xiii. 1–30, xv, xvi, xiii. 31–38, xiv, xvii.

---

[1] Edited by H. I. Bell and T. C. Skeat.

Among other minor re-arrangements it is possible iii. 22–30 originally stood after iii. 31–36. Moffatt inserts iii. 22–30 between ii. 12 and 13 ; xii. 44–50 in the middle of xii. 36 ; and reads xviii. 14, 19–24, 15–18, 25–27 to avoid the break in the narrative of Peter's denials.[1]

Sources and Influences. (1) The Witness who seems to be identical with the Beloved Disciple.

(2) The Synoptic tradition, at least in Mark and Luke.[2] It has already been noted that in the Synoptic tradition the Ministry lasted about one year, but according to John about two and a half years. If, however, the Cleansing of the Temple has been placed out of its true order and should come at the end of the Ministry after John xii. 19, then the Ministry according to this Gospel would be not much more than a year. But even in the Synoptic Gospels there are hints that Jesus had been to Jerusalem at other times besides the last week. In the dating of the Crucifixion John seems to be deliberately correcting the Synoptic account in favour of what many scholars accept as the original tradition.

(3) Harnack thought that the author used the Logos doctrine only in the Prologue, and then sub-

---

[1] This has some support in the Sinaitic Syriac. For the whole subject *v.* F. Warburton Lewis, *Disarrangements in the Fourth Gospel.*

[2] But *v.* p. 266.

stituted for it the conception of Jesus as the Only Begotten God (i. 18). But John's philosophy rests on the Incarnation, the Logos made flesh, and from the Prologue he passes naturally to the historical life of Jesus. Behind the Logos doctrine is the Old Testament teaching about the Word of God and the Rabbinic development of it as the divine Memra. But he has clearly been influenced also by Alexandrian philosophy, although he speaks of the Logos in terms which would have been impossible to Philo. For John the Logos is personal.

(4) Many parallels have been collected between the Johannine sayings and the Mandaean liturgies in which occur such phrases as " I am a Word," " a son of Words," " the Word of Life," " the Light of Life," " the worlds do not know thy Name nor understand thy Light." But such parallels show that Jewish and Christian beliefs may have influenced the development of Mandaism, but do not in any sense prove that Mandaism is a source of Christian doctrine.[1]

The Aims of the Author. John's answer to the question why he wrote his Gospel is, " These are written that ye may believe that Jesus is the Christ,

---

[1] *v.* W. F. Howard, *London Quarterly Review*, Jan. 1927 ; F. C. Burkitt, *J.T.S.*, April 1928 ; Vincent Taylor, *Hibbert Journal*, 1930.

the Son of God; and that believing ye may have
life in His name " (xx. 31). This aim influences his
choice of the " signs " and the " words " which he
records of Jesus. But he knows there are some
who do not believe, and one of his aims is to refute
them. (a) The Jews are the most prominent of
these, and much of the first half of the Gospel is
concerned with controversy with those " who believed not on him, though he had done so many
signs before them " (xii. 37). He does not accuse
them, as a Gentile might. " His very anger with
his own race is that of a Jew " (Lord Charnwood).
(b) There seem to have been some at Ephesus who
exalted the Baptist (cf. Acts xix. 1–7). John shows
the subordination of the Baptist to Jesus (iii. 30).
(c) The errors of Docetism are more fully exposed
in 1 John, but John's emphasis on the physical
details of the suffering of Jesus, on the reality of
His humanity, that the Logos " became flesh and
dwelt among us," and his avoidance of such words
as knowledge, wisdom, and faith, show that his
Gospel is anti-Gnostic. (d) He is aware of
certain dangers within the Church, especially of a
tendency to regard sacramental rites as having
magical efficacy, as in the Mystery religions; therefore he stresses the new birth as of water and of
the Spirit (iii. 5); and while he gives no account

of the institution of the Eucharist, he teaches the reality of feeding on the Bread of Life (ch. vi) and of abiding in Christ (ch. xv). His idea of the Church, which includes Samaritans and Greeks, reaches its climax in the High-priestly Prayer in ch. xvii. (e) Windisch [1] maintains that John wrote his Gospel not to supplement or interpret, but to supersede the others. He wrote one Gospel which was to be the Gospel. But it is difficult to see how his readers would understand parts of this Gospel (e.g. ch. vi), if they were not familiar with the Synoptic tradition; and we have no reason to believe that at the time when this Gospel was written any difficulty was created by the existence of four or more Gospels. (f) The author attempts a restatement of Christianity, a presentation not merely of the visual aspects of the life of Jesus on earth, but an interpretation of the historic facts, a resetting of them, not against the familiar Jewish background, but against the world, " a portrait of Jesus which would appeal and did appeal to the Hellenistic mind." Streeter claims that Christianity became a world religion, because in this Gospel it was given an expression which " was intellectually acceptable to the Greek and yet true to the Jewish thought of God as personal and as

---

[1] *Johannes und die Synoptiker.*

one." John presents the life of Jesus—an historical life—*sub specie eternitatis*, and shows that discipleship is as possible and as true for those of his generation as it had been for those who followed the Master in the days of His flesh ; that the blessing is equally sure for those who had not seen and yet had believed. One of the most illuminating sayings about this Gospel is that of Clement of Alexandria : " Last of all John, having observed that the bodily facts had been exhibited in the Gospels, urged by his friends and inspired by the Spirit, produced a spiritual Gospel." (Eus. *Hist. Eccles.*, vi. 14, 7.)

Date. If John has made use of Mark and Luke, his book must be later than A.D. 85. Since Ignatius knew it, the date cannot be put later than *c.* 115. It seems not unlikely that one of the fragments of papyri recently edited from the British Museum is a copy of a gospel not later than *c.* 110–130, and that the writer of this used John's Gospel. In *An Unpublished Fragment of the Fourth Gospel in the John Rylands Library*, the editor, C. H. Roberts, claims that this is part of a copy of the Gospel made between A.D. 130 and 150. Since this fragment belongs to Egypt and the Gospel to Ephesus, some time must be allowed for the Gospel to have become known so far away from the place of

origin. This is further evidence for dating the
Gospel of John not later than A.D. 110—more
probably A.D. 95–100.[1]

[1] If this is true, it shows how fantastic is the theory of Robert Eisler
that this Gospel was dictated by John the Elder to Marcion. This
theory he supports by a doubtful emendation of the corrupt *anti-
Marcionite Prologue* (in Latin) to the Gospel of John.

CHAPTER XXII

THE FIRST EPISTLE OF JOHN

The first Epistle of John so-called bears none of the usual marks of a letter. The author's name is not given, nor the destination to which it is to be sent. There are no greetings at the end. There are no definite personal, historical, or geographical allusions. This has led some scholars to call it a homily and to think it was addressed to the Christian Church generally. It is called an epistle, because tradition associated it with the name of John, along with other books in the New Testament, and there was no other type of book in the Canon with which it could be classed. It is more like a sermon (Streeter's name) than anything else, written by one who, from the position of authority which he held and from his age, could call his readers " little children." Because of the intense personal feeling, it seems best to treat it as a pastoral address to those whom the author knew well, in which he reminds them of what Christianity stands for in his experience, and of the dangers which threaten them from the erroneous teaching, which is anti-Christian and which will be fatal, if they do not heed his warning.

Canonicity. The epistle is cited by Polycarp, and mentioned in connexion with the Fourth Gospel in the Muratorian Fragment. Eusebius says Papias " used testimonies " from it, and he classes it among the books which were universally acknowledged.[1] It is better attested than any other of the Catholic Epistles.

The Epistle and the Gospel. The connexion with the Fourth Gospel is shown by the phraseology and doctrine. Such characteristic thoughts as the Incarnation of the Son of God,[2] the believer's abiding in God,[3] the love of the brethren,[4] the doctrine of eternal life, of the Christian believers as children of God ; the contrast of pairs of opposites—light and darkness, life and death, etc., are common to both. Although there are some differences of grammatical style, the linguistic similarities are far more striking than the divergencies.[5] There are no direct quotations from the Old Testament in the epistle : " the gospel is Christocentric and the epistle is Theocentric." [6] The Parousia is still expected in the near future. The conceptions of the epistle are on the whole more

---

[1] *Hist. Eccles.*, iii. 25.   [2] John i. 14, 1 John iv. 2.
[3] John xv, 1 John ii. 24.   [4] John xiii. 34, 1 John iii. 23.
[5] *v.* W. F. Howard, *The Fourth Gospel in Recent Criticism and Interpretation*, pp. 252–257.
[6] Cf. John vi. 56, xv. 4 ff, with 1 John iv, 15, 16.

commonplace and do not reach the heights of the Gospel.

Author. If the epistle was not by the writer of the Gospel, it was by another of the same circle.[1] Stanton sums up against that conclusion, " The respective individualities of two men—the one the author of the Epistle, the other of the Gospel, would have shewn themselves in more, and more strikingly distinct traits, than we have here. Men capable of producing either of these writings are not made, still less do they in life continue to be, so much alike in their modes of thought and speech, however strong their sympathy with one another, and however much one may have come under the influence of the other." [2] If John the Elder is the writer of the Gospel, then he is the writer of this letter.

Date. It is not clear whether he wrote this before the Gospel or after. Stanton argues that it is earlier than the Gospel, because no one who had written such a book would be likely afterwards to descend to the more ordinary conceptions of this epistle. But the epistle can hardly be understood apart from the Gospel. It seems perhaps more likely that this epistle is an attempt to make simpler and plainer the profound teaching of the Gospel.

[1] This view has the support of C. H. Dodd. *v. The Epistle of John and the Fourth Gospel, Bulletin of the John Rylands Library*, vol. 21, No. 1.

[2] *The Gospels as Historical Documents*, vol. iii, p. 105. *v.* W. F. Howard, *Christianity according to St. John*, p. 18.

The Purpose and Message of the Epistle. The false teaching which is here denounced is Docetism. For the Gnostic the Incarnation was impossible. It was explained as appearance only. Christ was a phantom. Cerinthus, who lived at Ephesus at the end of the first century, taught that Christ, the divine element, was united with the man Jesus at the Baptism, and left him before the Passion. Jesus was crucified, not Christ. During his Ministry it was Christ who spoke through the medium of Jesus. It is this form of heresy to which this epistle is a reply.

John's reply is that " Jesus Christ is come in the flesh," [1] is the central truth of Christianity. No man has ever seen God, but Jesus is the Son of God, and we have seen Him. And this is a part of our experience.[2] The historical Jesus is vital to Christianity. What He did and said is no secret. It can all be summed up in the word love—that is Christianity. The whole epistle is a variation on this theme, and can hardly be analysed.

The writer defines his purpose, " That which we have seen and heard declare we unto you also, that ye also may have fellowship with us ; yea, and our fellowship is with the Father, and with His Son Jesus Christ : and these things we write, that our

[1] iv. 2. [2] i. 1–4.

joy may be fulfilled " (i. 3, 4).   And again, " These things have I written unto you, that ye may know that ye have eternal life, even unto you that believe on the name of the Son of God " (v. 13).   Against the false gnosis of Cerinthianism he affirms that we know God in Jesus Christ.   " This is the true God, and eternal life.   *My* little children, guard yourselves from idols " [1]—i.e. from whatever gives you a distorted or false idea of God.

[1] v. 20, 21.

CHAPTER XXIII

THE SECOND AND THIRD EPISTLES OF JOHN

Canonicity. Considering the brevity of these two epistles, they are well attested. The Muratorian Fragment mentions two epistles of John as received in the Catholic Church, after referring to 1 John in connexion with the Gospel. That may mean 2 and 3 John, but possibly 1 and 2 John. Irenaeus quotes from 2 John twice. Clement of Alexandria recognizes 1 and 2 John as the work of John. Origen says these two short epistles are not accepted by all, and he never appears to quote from them. Eusebius says they were disputed and hints that they may be the work of the Elder John.[1] It was not until the end of the fourth century that their place in the Canon was secure, through the influence of Jerome and Augustine.

Author. The cumulative evidence from the style and diction of these two short letters proves they are written by the same hand that wrote the Gospel and 1 John.[2] The author calls himself in both

---

[1] ἑτέρου ὁμωνύμου. *Hist. Eccles.*, iii. 25.

[2] W. F. Howard, *The Fourth Gospel in Recent Criticism and Interpretation*, pp. 252–257.

"the elder" : he is evidently so well known that no other name is necessary. Surely such letters as these would not have been preserved, or at least not in the Canon, unless their author was one who was highly revered. The only one we know with this distinctive title is John the Elder, whom Papias mentions.

2 JOHN

Destination. The second Epistle is addressed " to the elect lady (ἐκλεκτῇ κυρίᾳ) and her children, whom I love in truth." Clement of Alexandria interpreted Electa as the name of a Babylonian lady, and he regarded her children (ver. 4) as Parthians. Augustine gives the title of the letter as " ad Parthos." Rendel Harris is almost alone among modern scholars in thinking that Electa is the name of a lady; he translates κυρίᾳ as " my dear."

ἡ ἐν βαβυλῶνι συνεκλεκτή is used in 1 Pet. v. 13 for " the Church in Babylon," and the word is used absolutely by Ignatius for a Church. So that we have good reason to believe that the " elect lady " means a Church, and this is borne out by the reference to the readers in the plural in vers. 6, 8, 10, 13. " The children of thine elect sister salute thee " (ver. 13) is a greeting from the Church in which the

Elder is. Possibly ἐκλεκτὴ κυρία (the elect lady) as a description of the Church may be due to the thought of the Church as the bride of ὁ Κύριος.[1]

Occasion. The purpose of this letter is to warn the Church that those are deceivers who " confess not that Jesus Christ cometh in the flesh " (ver. 7). The reference is to the Docetists. The author is anxious lest there should come to this Church and be given hospitality any wandering Christian teachers who were tainted with this false teaching. " If anyone cometh unto you, and bringeth not this teaching" (i.e. the teaching of Christ), " receive him not into *your* house, and give him no greeting: for he that giveth him greeting partaketh in his evil works " (vers. 10, 11). A similar warning is given about itinerant missionaries in the *Didache*.[2]

3 JOHN

Destination and Occasion. The letter is addressed to Gaius—an individual—not a church. Possibly he was an individual in the Church to which 2 John was written. The Elder implies that he had previously written to the Church (ver. 9), but Diotrephes, " who loveth to have the pre-eminence

[1] Cf. Apoc. xxi. 9; Eph. v. 25 ff.

[2] " Let every Apostle who comes to you be received as the Lord, but let him not stay more than one day, or if need be a second as well; but if he stay three days he is a false prophet " (xi. 4, 5).

among them," had apparently resented it. He had refused to receive the brethren whom the Elder had evidently commended to the Church, and he had cast out of the Church those who offered them hospitality. Apparently the brethren Diotrephes would not receive were on a preaching tour, and the Elder had commended them to be welcomed. Gaius is asked to show them hospitality.

What is the letter referred to in ver. 9? Possibly 2 John, but there is no mention of the Docetists in 3 John. 2 John does not refer to Diotrephes, nor say anything about the reception of the missionaries which we are to suppose was the subject of the letter. Gaius is not to be identified with any other Gaius[1] mentioned in the New Testament, nor is Demetrius to be identified with the Demetrius at Ephesus[2] or the Demas who forsook Paul.[3] This Demetrius may have been the leader of the itinerant missionaries whom the Elder commends. Diotrephes may have been exalted with spiritual pride (ver. 9) by the Gnosticism against which the Elder had written a warning in 2 John. Streeter rather supposes that he resented the " modernism " of the Elder, and those whom he had sent : that he also rebelled against the interference of the Elder,

[1] Acts xix. 29 ; Rom. xvi. 23. [2] Acts xix. 24.
[3] 2 Tim. iv. 10.

because he had become bishop of the Church in the monarchical sense, and used his authority to excommunicate those who showed hospitality to the Elder's friends. John the Elder, Streeter thinks, who speaks with authority for the Church whence he writes (2 John 13) and who writes as one claiming authority (2 John 4), was himself a bishop and of a Church which claims precedence over others. The evidence seems to point to the Elder being bishop of Ephesus, the mother Church of Asia, and in a sense he might be described as archbishop.[1]

[1] *The Primitive Church*, pp. 83–89.

CHAPTER XXIV

THE REVELATION OF JOHN

Unity. In form this book is an encyclical letter to the " seven Churches which are in Asia." But the epistolary form is exchanged for the apocalyptic, in which the greater part of the book is written. Since literary criticism has illuminated so many books in the New Testament, it was natural that many scholars should have attempted to solve the difficulties which this book presents by searching for sources and tracing the hands of compilers. It has been suggested that the " Letters to the Churches " are by one hand and the rest of the book by another : that it is a compilation of two or more Jewish apocalypses, which belong to different dates, and which have been pieced together by a redactor. Vischer supposed one Jewish apocalypse worked over by a Christian. But it has become widely recognized that the book is a unity, that it was conceived by one mind and written by one hand. R. H. Charles[1] thinks there is evidence that John wrote the " Letters to the Churches " some time before he wrote the Apocalypse, but that he then

[1] *Commentary on Revelation* (International Critical Commentary).

edited them as a message for the universal Church in a book, in which he has incorporated many fragments of earlier apocalypses. But these he has woven into the fabric of his visions very much as the imagery of the Old Testament prophets was woven into the conceptions of the apocalyptists. In other apocalyptic passages in the New Testament (e.g. Mark xiii and 2 Thess. ii. 1–12) the writers are adapting Jewish material of an earlier date, and interpreting it in the light of the Christian expectation. The author of the Apocalypse is doing the same on a larger scale. He uses his sources with such freedom and literary skill that it is almost impossible for literary criticism to disentangle them, since he has worked them up into a " form which is permeated by his own personality " (Swete); and rigid consistency is the last thing to be expected in a work of this character. He is in the line of the prophets : where they said, " Thus saith Yahveh," he says, " I saw, and behold a door opened in heaven " (iv. 1).

The Old Testament prophets and the later Jewish apocalyptists experienced dreams and visions in sleep and in waking moments, which brought them a revelation of God. Psychology finds many parallels from other religions ; but the value of such experiences depends upon the level of the religious faith which they express, and of the moral duties which they commend. The seer is trying to express " unspeakable things," [1] which he had seen in his ecstasies ; he can only use images which are symbolic. But the seer of these visions is a literary artist, and in his waking moments he has arranged his thoughts, elaborated his allegories, worked over the fragments of Old Testament prophecy and Jewish apocalypse, until the whole has a literary form which makes his book a unity.

Outline. There is no general agreement as to the plan of the book. Some divide it into acts and scenes, others can find in it no movement, only repetition. Charles maintains that the action is continuous, but that this is obscured by derangements and interpolations due to an incompetent redactor. The following outline is based upon the analysis of Charles.

1. The Prologue (i. 1–3).
2. The Apocalypse in seven parts (i. 4–xxii. 5).
3. The Epilogue (xxi. 5–8, xxii. 6–21).

The Apocalypse itself is in seven parts :

1. The Prologue on earth (i. 4–20).
2. The " Letters to the Seven Churches," which show the apparent failure of the cause of God on earth—which is the problem of the book (chs. ii. iii).

[1] 2 Cor. xii. 4.

3. The Prologue in heaven—the vision of God and of the Lamb (chs. iv, v).

4. A series of Judgments : (*a*) The Seals (ch. vi). (*b*) The Trumpets (chs. viii, ix, xii, xiii). (*c*) The Bowls—followed by the doom of Rome ; the victory of Christ ; and the chaining of Satan for one thousand years (xv. 5–xx. 3).

The omitted chapters form three parentheses :

(1) Ch. vii.   The marking of the Saints to prevent them from being affected by the judgment of the Trumpets.

(2) Chs. x–xi, in which it is shown that the hour for which the martyrs prayed has come, and that although what follows seems to be the triumph of Satan, the real result is the Coming of Christ.

(3) Ch. xiv.   The visions of the Church Triumphant and of the Judgment of Rome.

5. The Reign of Christ for one thousand years : the final attack and destruction of the powers of evil (xxi. 9–xxii. 2, 14, 15, 17, xx. 4–10).

6. The Last Judgment (xx. 11–15).

7. The New Jerusalem (xxi. 1–5a, xxii. 3–5).

The few verses omitted are editorial interpolations.

In the traditional order of the last three chapters after heaven and earth have been destroyed, the heavenly Jerusalem is described as standing on the old earth, and evil still exists outside it,[1] although all who are not redeemed have been destroyed.[2] Charles thinks there are two cities and that an editor has caused confusion in the text. A new city appears on the site of Jerusalem in which Christ reigns for a thousand years (xxi. 9–xxii. 2). At the end of that time Satan is unchained and is defeated and cast into the lake of fire (xx. 7–10). The general Resurrection and the Last Judgment follow, and all who were outside the Heavenly Jerusalem are condemned to the lake of fire (xx. 14). The Messianic Kingdom comes to an end when Christ is triumphant and death is subdued (xx. 14). Then a New Heaven and a New Earth appear and a New City. The New City cannot be described; it belongs to the new conditions of life when Christ shall deliver up the Kingdom to God, and God is all in all (cf. 1 Cor. xv. 23–28).

Authorship. 1. Unlike Jewish apocalypses which are pseudonymous, the author writes under his own name, John.[3]

2. This John is not the writer of the Gospel and Epistles. Although both are connected by tradition with Ephesus, and both were most likely Jews, this John does not call himself Apostle or Elder, although either title would have given his words

---

[1] xxii. 15. [2] xx. 15. [3] i. 1–4.

additional authority. Dionysius of Alexandria and Eusebius say the author of the Apocalypse is John the Elder, and they believe John the Apostle to have written the Gospel. The writer of the Gospel does not mention himself by name. The writer of the Apocalypse calls himself John, but does not identify himself with the " Beloved Disciple." But the evidence of the style and diction and theological outlook is convincing proof that the writer of the Apocalypse did not write the Gospel. Out of about 900 words in both books, fewer than half are common.[1] The Greek of the Gospel is idiomatic ; that of the Apocalypse is so full of solecisms that Charles has written a special Grammar for it. Where both books use similar phrases, the meaning is generally different, and the concrete symbolism of the Advent and Judgment is far removed from the spiritual conception of the Gospel. It has been suggested that the Evangelist wrote the Apocalypse twenty years or so before the Gospel and his Greek improved. But the evidence is too strong against identity of authorship.[2]

3. If " the Elder " is the author of the Gospel, it

---

[1] E.g. The Gospel uses πιστεύειν, ἀγαπᾶν, ἀγάπη very frequently—they are rare in the Apocalypse. The Lamb is ὁ ἀμνός in the Gospel (twice), τὸ ἀρνίον in the Apocalypse (twenty-nine times). ἀλήθεια, so common in the Gospel, is not in the Apocalypse.

[2] v. Jülich r-Fascher, Einleitung in das Neue Testament, s. 259–261.

is still unlikely that the author of the Apocalypse is John, the son of Zebedee, for the reasons already given. If John the Apostle was martyred,[1] and never went to Ephesus, then he cannot have been the prophet who wrote the Apocalypse, for it was not written till after A.D. 70.

4. The author was a Jew who lived in Ephesus and was exiled to Patmos. To distinguish him from John the Apostle and John the Elder, Charles calls him John the Seer.[2] He was steeped in the language of the Old Testament as well as in the earlier apocalyptic literature ; and although Greek was not the language in which he habitually thought he was far from being illiterate.

Date. Three dates have been suggested :

1. After the persecution in the reign of Nero, but before the Fall of Jerusalem. (*a*) Jerome quotes Tertullian to the effect that John suffered exile in Patmos in Nero's reign. (*b*) In Apoc. xi. 1 the Temple and city are spoken of as if still standing. (*c*) Those who think the author was John the Apostle date it some twenty or twenty-five years earlier than the Gospel.

2. Vespasian's reign, because Vespasian is prob-

---

[1] Charles is convinced by the evidence, but *v*. J. H. Bernard, *Commentary on St. John* (International Critical Commentary), pp. xxxv–xlv.

[2] He calls his book a prophecy, i. 3, x. 11, xxii. 7, 9, 10, 18.

ably the sixth Emperor referred to in xvii. 10. (This may have been written in Vespasian's reign and adapted later.)

3. Domitian's reign. The condition of the Churches is later than Paul's time. This is seen in the references to the deterioration of the Churches in Ephesus [1] and in Laodicea.[2] The writer denounces the Nicolaitans,[3] who were for compromise between the claims of Christianity and of the State religion, Emperor worship. The persecution of Nero's reign was confined to Rome; only in Domitian's reign did it extend to Asia. The background seems to be the time when the Emperor's demand for divine honours, his widespread use of informers, and his fiendish fury against the Christians established a reign of terror in his later years. Although part of the book may have been written earlier, the references to the Nero redivivus legend make it most probable that the book in its present form was written in A.D. 90–96. The conception of Anti-Christ, which had been already fused with the dragon myth of Beliar in 2 Thess. ii. 3, is in this book fused with the expectation that Nero was not dead, but was in hiding among the Parthians, and would presently reappear at the head of the Parthian hosts, whom the Romans had good cause

[1] ii. 1–6. [2] iii. 14–19. [3] ii. 15.

to fear. But he would appear not as the three pretenders who claimed to be Nero in the ten years that followed his death, but as the Beast [1] from the abyss, a supernatural monster (xvi. 12–14).

Methods of Interpretation. 1. Mystical. The Alexandrian scholars, Augustine, and many others, have interpreted the visions of the book as allegories, with results which are curious but which have not always made for edification.

2. Historical. The book gives no diagram of human history, so that it is to be understood as a prophecy of events which are to take place in the history of the world, and which those who understand it aright can foresee. The visions relate to things contemporary with the writer and his readers; e.g. the state of the Seven Churches; and to future events in so far as they will issue from them. From ch. v to the end is a description of things which the writer expected would take place immediately, and by which human history would come to an end. The author did not look beyond his own age, but inasmuch as his visions are an expression of the truth that all human history is in God's hands, they have in a sense been fulfilled many times over.

---

[1] The number of the Beast 666 supports the identification with Nero redivivus. The value of the letters נרון קסר numerically is 666; if the final ן is omitted, the value is 616, a v.l. in Apoc. xiii. 18.

Purpose and Message. The theme of the apocalyptic writers is the " Day of the Lord," which, when it dawned, would reveal that there was a divine Ruler, who was supreme over the world of nature and over all the political movements among the nations. John, the Seer, differs from the Jewish apocalyptists in that they foretold the coming of the Messiah; he has a message from the Messiah Who has come; Who has won the victory over man's last enemy, death; Who bears the marks now of His suffering, but Who is exalted to be the Lord of Lords and King of Kings. He writes to assure his readers that God's final judgment is at hand, when He will vindicate His saints. The Seven Churches represent the Christian Church, Rome represents the power of this world, " the negation of God erected into a system." Caesar or Christ was the issue before his readers, and he encourages them to resist unto blood the blasphemous claims of the Roman Emperors to divine worship. The issue of the coming conflict will be the triumph of Christ and the blessedness of the redeemed. But he warns his readers that before that consummation there will be a series of events in which the struggle between good and evil will grow more intense, and he contemplates that the persecution will mean the universal martyrdom of Christians. But the intensity of the struggle on earth is because

Satan has been defeated and cast out of heaven. The victory, already won in heaven against all the spiritual host of darkness, will be finally accomplished on earth. Although in the cries for vengeance, and in the lurid description of the horrors which it is the purpose of God to let loose upon the world, there is much that is below the Christian level, in the belief of the writer in the final triumph of spiritual forces, and in his vision of the Heavenly City, he has inspired with hope many generations of those who are persecuted for righteousness' sake.[1] And if Charles is right in his re-arrangement of the last chapters, then the Seer looks even beyond the Heavenly Jerusalem, which in a sense answers to the hopes of others besides Christians, an ideal which men have represented in many different ways. He has seen a vision of another city, the New Jerusalem, which will be the spiritual and therefore permanent completion of dreams which can never be realized on earth, when God shall be with His people and death shall be no more (xxi. 1–5a).

[1] v. E. F. Scott, *The Book of Revelation*, pp. 150 ff.

BIBLIOGRAPHY

GENERAL

The Abingdon Bible Commentary.

C. Gore : *A New Commentary on Holy Scripture.*

T. W. Manson : *A Companion to the Bible.*

A. S. Peake : *Commentary on the Bible.*

A. Deissmann : *The New Testament in the Light of Modern Research.*

C. H. Dodd : *The Apostolic Preaching and its Developments.*

P. Feine : *Einleitung in das Neue Testament.*

Edgar J. Goodspeed : *New Chapters in New Testament Study.*

M. R. James : *The Apocryphal New Testament.*

Maurice Jones : *The New Testament in the Twentieth Century.*

Jülicher-Fascher : *Einleitung in das Neue Testament.*

A. M. Hunter : *Introducing the New Testament.*

K. and S. Lake : *An Introduction to the New Testament.*

A. H. McNeile : *Introduction to the New Testament.*

G. Milligan : *The New Testament Documents.*

J. Moffatt : *The Approach to the New Testament.*
Introduction to the Literature of the New Testament.

A. Nairne : *The Faith of the New Testament.*

A. S. Peake : *A Critical Introduction to the New Testament.*

C. A. Anderson Scott : *Living Issues in the New Testament.*

Canon and Text

C. R. Gregory : *Canon and Text of the New Testament.*
A. von Harnack : *The Origin of the New Testament.*
Sir F. G. Kenyon : *The Text of the Greek Bible.*
K. Lake : *The Text of the New Testament.*
A. Souter : *The Text and Canon of the New Testament.*

The Gospels

F. C. Burkitt : *The Earliest Sources for the Life of Jesus.*
Jesus Christ : an Historical Outline.
The Gospel History and its Transmission.
C. H. Dodd : *History and the Gospel.*
W. Fairweather : *The Background of the Gospels.*
A. von Harnack : *The Date of the Synoptic Gospels and Acts.*
J. Rendel Harris : *Testimonies I, II.*
R. H. Lightfoot : *History and Interpretation in the Gospels.*
Locality and Doctrine in the Gospels.
T. W. Manson : *The Teaching of Jesus.*
W. Sanday (Ed.) : *Oxford Studies in the Synoptic Problem.*
E. F. Scott : *The Validity of the Gospel Record.*
V. H. Stanton : *The Gospels as Historical Documents.*
B. H. Streeter : *The Four Gospels.*
V. Taylor : *The Gospels.*
C. C. Torrey : *The Four Gospels.*
Our Translated Gospels.
R. V. G. Tasker : *The Nature and Purpose of the Gospels.*
B. W. Bacon : *Studies in Matthew.*
The Gospel of Mark.
Matthew Black : *An Aramaic Approach to the Gospels and Acts.*

C. F. Burney : *The Aramaic Origin of the Fourth Gospel.*

G. D. Kilpatrick : *The Origins of the Gospel according to St. Matthew.*

H. J. Cadbury : *The Making of Luke—Acts.*
The Style and Literary Method of Luke.

J. E. Carpenter : *The Johannine Writings.*

P. Gardner-Smith : *Saint John and the Synoptic Gospels.*

A. von Harnack : *The Sayings of Jesus.*
Luke the Physician.

Sir Edwyn Hoskyns : *The Fourth Gospel* (2 vols.).

W. F. Howard : *The Fourth Gospel in Recent Criticism and Interpretation.*
Christianity according to St. John.

E. F. Scott : *The Fourth Gospel.*

R. H. Strachan : *The Fourth Gospel.*

V. Taylor : *Behind the Third Gospel.*

W. Temple : *Readings in St. John's Gospel* (2 vols.).

FORM-CRITICISM

R. Bultmann : *Die Geschichte der Synoptischen Tradition.*

Martin Dibelius : *From Tradition to Gospel.*
Gospel Criticism and Christology.
A Fresh Approach to the New Testament and Early Christian Literature.

B. S. Easton : *The Gospel before the Gospels.*

E. Fascher : *Die Formgeschichtliche Methode.*

F. C. Grant : *Form-criticism : A Translation of the Study of the Synoptic Gospels,* by R. Bultmann, *and of Primitive Christianity in the Light of Gospel Research,* by Karl Kundsin.

E. B. Redlich : *Form-Criticism.*

K. L. Schmidt : *Der Rahmen der Geschichte Jesu.*
Vincent Taylor : *The Formation of the Gospel Tradition.*

ACTS AND EPISTLES

F. C. Burkitt : *Christian Beginnings.*
A. C. Clark : *The Acts of the Apostles.*
A. Deissmann : *Paul.*
C. H. Dodd : *The Mind of Paul.*
G. S. Duncan : *St. Paul's Ephesian Ministry.*
W. Fairweather : *The Background of the Epistles.*
F. J. Foakes Jackson : *The Life of St. Paul.*
F. J. Foakes Jackson and Kirsopp Lake (Edd.) : *The Beginnings of Christianity* (5 vols.).
T. R. Glover : *Paul of Tarsus.*
A. von Harnack : *The Date of the Acts and of the Synoptic Gospels.*
   The Acts of the Apostles.
Sir Robert Falconer : *The Pastoral Epistles.*
P. N. Harrison : *The Problem of the Pastoral Epistles.*
A. M. Hunter : *Paul and his Predecessors.*
W. L. Knox : *St. Paul and the Church of the Gentiles.*
Kirsopp Lake : *The Earlier Epistles of St. Paul.*
A. H. McNeile : *St. Paul : His Life, Letters and Christian Doctrine.*
Sir W. Ramsay : *Letters to the Seven Churches in Asia.*
   St. Paul the Traveller and Roman Citizen.
C. A. Anderson Scott : *Footnotes to St. Paul.*
   St. Paul, the Man and the Teacher.
E. F. Scott : *The Epistle to the Hebrews.*
   The Book of Revelation.
B. H. Streeter : *The Primitive Church.*

C. C. Torrey : *The Composition and Date of Acts*.

Johannes Weiss : *The History of Primitive Christianity* (2 vols.).

COMMENTARIES

The Cambridge Greek Testament, of which the more recent volumes are St. Matthew (B. T. D. Smith), St. Mark (Plummer), St. Luke (Luce), Romans (Parry), 1 Corinthians (Parry), Ephesians (Murray), Hebrews (Nairne).

The Clarendon Bible. The following volumes have appeared : St. Matthew (Green), St. Mark (Blunt), St. Luke (Balmforth), Acts (Blunt), Romans (Kirk), Corinthians (Evans), Galatians (Blunt), Hebrews (Narborough).

The Expositors' Greek Testament (5 vols.).

The International Critical Commentary, of which the more recent volumes are : St. John (Bernard), Galatians (Burton), Pastoral Epistles (Lock), Hebrews (Moffatt), Revelation (Charles).

Macmillan's Commentaries. Among the best of the older commentaries are those by J. B. Lightfoot on Galatians, Philippians, Colossians, by J. Armitage Robinson on Ephesians, by G. Milligan on Thessalonians, by B. F. Westcott on Hebrews. The most recent volumes in this series are St. Matthew (McNeile), St. Luke (Creed), 1 Peter (Selwyn).

The Moffatt New Testament Commentary. The following volumes have appeared : St. Matthew (T. H. Robinson), St. Mark (Branscomb), St. Luke (Manson), St. John (Macgregor), Acts (Foakes Jackson), Romans (Dodd), 1 Corinthians (Moffatt), 2 Corinthians (Strachan), Galatians (Duncan), Colossians, Philemon, Ephesians (E. F. Scott), Philippians (Michael), The Pastoral Epistles (E. F. Scott), Hebrews (T. H. Robinson), General Epistles (Moffatt), The Johannine Epistles (C. H. Dodd), Revelation (Martin Kiddle).

The Westminster Commentaries. The most recent volumes are : St. Mark (Rawlinson), Thessalonians (Bicknell), St. Peter and St. Jude (Wand).

ADDITIONAL NOTES

CHAPTER I, PAGE 12

P. N. Harrison in *Polycarp's Two Epistles to the Philippians* has shown good reasons for believing that Polycarp's Epistle consists of two letters. Of these, ch. xiii is the earlier and belongs to the year of Ignatius' Martyrdom, *c.* A.D. 115. The other letter is ch. i–xii, which show Polycarp's knowledge of most of the books of the New Testament. This was written *c.* A.D. 135.

CHAPTER IV, PAGE 54

It is possible that Paul's second visit to Jerusalem mentioned in Gal. ii. 1–10 is not recorded at all in Acts, but that it took place after Barnabas and Saul had been set apart by the Church in Antioch for missionary work, Acts xiii. 2. They received the imprimatur of the Church in Jerusalem before they set sail. That would date the visit a year or two before the Council of Acts xv. It was after this first missionary journey that Peter withdrew from table-fellowship with the Gentiles in Antioch, Gal. ii. 11–14. The controversy which Peter's action provoked was the immediate cause of the Council at Jerusalem (Acts xv), the decisions of which regulated table-fellowship between Jew and Gentile. The controversy over circumcision arose later, for it appears as a live issue in those letters of Paul which belong to the third missionary journey (*v.* T. W. Manson, *The Problem of the Epistle to the Galatians from the "Bulletin of the John Rylands Library,"* vol. 24, No. 1, April 1940). This explanation (which is not without its own difficulties), like some other explanations, suggests that Luke in his account of the Council in Acts xv has combined two questions, which were the subjects of discussion on two different occasions.

CHAPTER XVIII, PAGE 215

The beginning of the Gospel of Mark, as we know it, is so awkward, grammatically, that Spitta suggested that the true beginning has been lost and verses 1–3 are a patchwork. Probably, therefore, the Gospel is defective at the beginning and at the end. These were the most vulnerable parts of an ancient papyrus whether in the roll or the papyrus form (*v.* T. W. Manson, *The Foundation of the Synoptic Tradition : The Gospel of Mark from the "Bulletin of the John Rylands Library,"* vol. 28, No. 1, March 1944).

CHAPTER XIX, PAGE 219

T. W. Manson has made out a strong case for thinking that (*a*) in his statement about the Logia Papias was referring to Q ; (*b*) Matthew composed Q ; (*c*) our Greek Matthew was translated into Aramaic at a very early date for Jewish Christians in Palestine and Syria ; (*d*) " the name of Matthew, which had been mistakenly transferred from Q to the first Gospel, stuck, and continued to stick, until scientific study of the relations between the Gospels made the hypothesis of an original Hebrew Matthew untenable." (v. T. W. Manson, *The Gospel according to St. Matthew from the " Bulletin of the John Rylands Library,"* vol. 29, No. 2, February 1946).

THE OLDEST ANTI-MARCIONITE GOSPEL PROLOGUES

There is no Prologue to Matthew extant. The other three are found in thirty-eight different MSS. from the fifth to the tenth century. They are all in Latin, but that to Luke is found also in Greek in two MSS. There is good ground for thinking that these Latin Prologues are all translations from an original Greek, made probably in Africa at the end of the third century. The Johannine Prologue is undoubtedly corrupt, but no emendation has won wide acceptance.

These Prologues must have been written after Papias and before Irenaeus, probably between A.D. 160 and 180.

For a discussion of the significance of the Prologues, *v. The Anti-Marcionite Prologues of the Gospels*, W. F. Howard, *Expository Times*, vol. xlvii, No. 12.

1. THE ANTI-MARCIONITE PROLOGUE TO MARK

. . . declared Mark, who was called colobodactylus (the man with the docked finger), because he had small fingers in proportion to the height of his body. He was Peter's interpreter, and he wrote his Gospel after Peter's death in the region of Italy.

2. THE ANTI-MARCIONITE PROLOGUE TO LUKE

Luke was of Antioch in Syria, a physician by profession, who had been a disciple of the Apostles, and who after wards accompanied Paul until his martyrdom. He served the Lord continually. He had neither wife nor children. He fell asleep at the age of 84 in Boeotia, full of Holy Spirit.

When there were already Gospels in existence (that according to Matthew written down in Judaea, and that according to Mark in Italy), this man (Luke) impelled by Holy Spirit composed his whole Gospel in Achaea; shewing by his preface this very fact, that before him other (Gospels) had been written, and that it was necessary for the sake of the believers from among the Gentiles to set forth an accurate record of the Christian dispensation, so that they should not be disturbed by Jewish tales and should not miss the truth because they were deceived by heretical and vain imaginings. So at the beginning of the Gospel we have handed down to us as being most essential (the account of) the birth of John; who is the beginning of the Gospel; who was the forerunner of the Lord; and who shared in the preparation of the people, in the introduction of baptism and in the fellowship of suffering. (*The translation here follows the Latin and not the Greek, with Harnack's approval.*) Of this dispensation a prophet (Malachi, *according to the Latin*) makes mention.

And at a later date the same Luke wrote the Acts of the Apostles. And afterwards John the Apostle, one of the Twelve, wrote the Apocalypse, and after that the Gospel.

3. THE ANTI-MARCIONITE PROLOGUE TO JOHN

The Gospel of John was published and given to the Churches by John, while he was still in the body, as

Papias, called Hieropolitanus, the beloved disciple of John, related in his Five Expository Books. Indeed he (Papias) wrote down the Gospel, while John accurately dictated. But the heretic Marcion, when he had been condemned by him (Papias), because he held opposed views, was expelled by John. He (Marcion) had indeed brought documents or letters to him (Papias) from the brethren who were in Pontus.

OTHER EARLY WITNESSES TO THE BOOKS OF THE NEW TESTAMENT

IRENAEUS

Matthew produced a written Gospel among the Hebrews in their own tongue, while Peter and Paul were preaching the Gospel in Rome and founding the Church. After their death (*or* departure) Mark, the disciple and interpreter of Peter, himself too handed down to us in writing the things which Peter had proclaimed. Luke, too, the follower of Paul, committed to writing the Gospel preached by him (Paul). Afterwards John, the disciple of the Lord, who also lay on his breast, himself also published his Gospel, while living at Ephesus in Asia.

(Eusebius, *Hist. Eccles.*, v. 8.)

THE MURATORIAN FRAGMENT

. . . but at some he was present, and so he set them down.

The third book of the Gospel, that according to Luke, was compiled in his own name in order by Luke the physician, when, after Christ's ascension, Paul had taken him to be with him like a student of law. Yet neither did he see the Lord in the flesh; and he too as he was able to ascertain [events, so set them down]. So he began his story from the birth of John.

The fourth of the Gospels [was written by] John, one of the disciples. When exhorted by his fellow-disciples and bishops, he said, " Fast with me this day for three days ; and what may be revealed to any of us let us relate it to one another." The same night it was revealed to Andrew, one of the apostles, that John was to write all things in his own name, and they were all to certify.

And therefore, though various elements are taught in the several books of the Gospels, yet it makes no difference to the faith of believers, since by one guiding Spirit all things are declared in all of them concerning the Nativity, the Passion, the Resurrection, the conversation with his disciples and his two comings, the first in lowliness and contempt, which has come to pass, the second glorious with royal power, which is to come.

What marvel therefore if John so firmly sets forth each statement in his Epistle, too, saying of himself, " What we have seen with our eyes and heard with our ears and our hands have handled, these things we have written to you " ? For so he declares himself not an eyewitness and a hearer only, but a writer of all the marvels of the Lord in order.

The Acts, however, of all the Apostles are written in one book. Luke puts it shortly to the most excellent Theophilus, that the several things were done in his own presence, as he also plainly shows by leaving out the passion of Peter, and also the departure of Paul from town on his journey to Spain.

The Epistles, however, of Paul themselves make plain to those who wish to understand it, what epistles were

sent by him, and from what place and for what cause.
He wrote at some length first of all to the Corinthians,
forbidding schisms and heresies ; next to the Galatians,
forbidding circumcision ; then to the Romans, impress-
ing on them the plan of the Scriptures, and also that
Christ is the first principle of them, concerning which
severally it is [not] necessary for us to discuss, since the
blessed Apostle Paul himself, following the order of his
predecessor John, writes only by name to seven churches
in the following order—to the Corinthians a first, to the
Ephesians a second, to the Philippians a third, to the
Colossians a fourth, to the Galatians a fifth, to the
Thessalonians a sixth, to the Romans a seventh ; whereas, although for the sake of admonition there is a second
to the Corinthians and to the Thessalonians, yet one
Church is recognized as being spread over the entire
world. For John, too, in the Apocalypse, though he
writes to seven churches, yet speaks to all. Howbeit to
Philemon one, to Titus one, and to Timothy two were
put in writing from personal inclination and attachment,
to be in honour, however, with the Catholic Church for
the ordering of the ecclesiastical mode of life. There is
current also one to the Laodicenes, another to the
Alexandrians, [both] forged in Paul's name to suit the
heresy of Marcion, and several others which cannot be
received into the Catholic Church ; for it is not fitting
that gall be mixed with honey.

The Epistle of Jude no doubt, and the couple bearing
the name of John, are accepted in the Catholic [Church] ;
and the Wisdom written by the friends of Solomon in
his honour. The Apocalypse also of John, and of Peter

[one Epistle, which] only we receive ; [there is also a second] which some of our friends will not have read in the Church. (*These lines have been amended.*) But the Shepherd was written quite lately in our times by Hermas, while his brother Pius, the bishop, was sitting in the chair of the church of the city of Rome ; and therefore it ought indeed to be read, but it cannot to the end of time be publicly read in the Church to the people, either among the prophets, who are complete in number, or among the Apostles. . . .

(Translation by H. M. Gwatkin in *Selections from Early Christian Writers.*)

CLEMENT OF ALEXANDRIA

In the Hypotyposes, to sum up the matter briefly, he has given us abridged accounts of all the canonical Scriptures, not even omitting those that are disputed, I mean the Epistle of Jude and the other General Epistles, the Epistle of Barnabas and the so-called Revelation of Peter. But the Epistle to the Hebrews he says was written by Paul to the Hebrews in the Hebrew language, but that Luke carefully translated it and published it to the Greeks. That is why the same character of style and phraseology is found in this Epistle as in the Acts. " But probably the title, Paul the Apostle, was not prefixed to it." For he says, " Writing to the Hebrews, who had imbibed a prejudice against him and suspected him, he quite wisely did not put them off at the beginning by giving his name." Later he observes, " But now as the blessed Presbyter used to say, ' Since the Lord, who was the apostle of the Almighty, was sent to the Hebrews,

Paul, by reason of his inferiority as sent to the Gentiles, did not subscribe himself as an apostle of the Hebrews; both out of reverence for the Lord, and because he wrote out of his abundance to the Hebrews, as a herald and apostle of the Gentiles.'" Again in the same book Clement has set down the tradition of the oldest presbyters about the order of the Gospels in this way. He said that those which had the genealogies were written first, and that the Gospel according to Mark was occasioned in this way. "When Peter had proclaimed the word publicly in Rome, and under the influence of the Spirit had declared the Gospel, the great number who were present requested Mark, who had followed him for a long time and remembered what he had said, to reduce his discourses to writing. And Mark, after composing the Gospel, gave it to those who asked him to do this. And when Peter understood this, he neither hindered it nor encouraged it directly. But last of all John, having observed that the bodily facts had been exhibited in the Gospels, urged by his friends, and inspired by the Spirit, produced a spiritual Gospel."

(Eusebius, *Hist. Eccles.*, vi. 14.)

ORIGEN

In the first book of his commentaries on the Gospel according to Matthew, keeping the Canon of the Church, he attests that he knows four Gospels only, writing as follows : " As I have learned in tradition about the four Gospels, which are the only undisputed Gospels in the Church of God throughout the world: the Gospel according to Matthew, who was once a tax-collector and

after an apostle of Jesus Christ, was written first.   He
published it for converts from Judaism, and it was composed in Hebrew.   The Gospel according to Mark was
second.   He wrote it as Peter explained to him.   Peter
acknowledged Mark as his son in his General Epistle,
saying, ' She that is in Babylon, elect together with you,
saluteth you ; so doth Mark my son.'   The Gospel
according to Luke was third, the Gospel praised by Paul.
Luke wrote it for the converts from the Gentiles.   The
Gospel according to John was last of all."   And in the
fifth volume of his commentaries on the Gospel according to John the same author says this about the Epistles
of the Apostles : " Now he who was well fitted to be a
minister of the New Covenant, a minister not of the
letter but of the spirit, Paul, who having spread the
Gospel ' from Jerusalem and round about even unto
Illyricum ' did not even write to all the churches to
which he preached, but even to those to which he wrote
he sent only a few lines.   But Peter, upon whom the
Church of Christ is built, against which the gates of
Hades shall not prevail, has left one undisputed Epistle.
Suppose that he has left also a second Epistle—for this
is disputed.   What must I say about him who reclined
upon the breast of Jesus, John, who has left one Gospel,
acknowledging that he could have written so many that
not even the world could contain them ?   And he wrote
also the Apocalypse, having been commanded to keep
silent and not to write of the voices of the seven thunders.
He has left an Epistle also consisting of very few lines.
Suppose he has left also a second and a third Epistle ;
for not all agree that these are genuine ; but both to-

gether do not consist of a hundred lines." Further in addition to this he adds as follows about the Epistle to the Hebrews in his homilies upon it : " The style of the diction of the Epistle entitled ' To the Hebrews ' is not rude like the language of the Apostle, who acknowledged himself ' to be rude in speech,' that is, in expression ; but the Epistle in composition and diction is purer Greek, as everyone who is skilled to distinguish differences of expression will acknowledge. And again that the thoughts of the Epistle are admirable and not inferior to the books acknowledged to be apostolic every one who carefully studies the apostolic text will acknowledge to be true." To this he adds later : " If I gave my opinion I should say that the thoughts are those of the Apostle ; but the expression and composition are those of one who remembered the Apostle's teachings, and who wrote down at his leisure what had been said by his teacher. Therefore if any church holds this Epistle as Paul's, let it be commended also for this ; for not without reason have the ancients handed it down as Paul's. But who wrote the Epistle in truth God knows. The statement of some who have gone before us is that Clement, who was bishop of the Romans, wrote the Epistle, and of others that Luke wrote it, Luke who wrote the Gospel and Acts."

(Eusebius, *Hist. Eccles.*, vi. 25.)

EUSEBIUS

Nevertheless of all the followers of the Lord, Matthew and John alone have left us memoirs. Even they, report

says, came to write (their Gospels) under compulsion.
For Matthew, having first preached to Hebrews, when he
was intending to go to other nations, also committed to
writing in his native tongue the Gospel that bears his
name ; and so to those from whom he was parting made
up for the lack of his presence by the written book.
And when Mark and Luke had already published the
Gospels that bear their names, they say that John, who
all this time had preached the Gospel but not written it,
at last also proceeded to write it for this reason.   When
the three Gospels which had previously been written
had been distributed to him, as to all, they say that he
admitted them and testified to their truth but he said,
there was wanting in the written narrative only the
account of the things done by Christ at first and in the
beginning of his proclamation of the Gospel.   And the
statement was true.   For it is clear that the other three
evangelists had a general view, and wrote only of the
things done by the Saviour in the one year after the
imprisonment of John the Baptist, and they signified
this in the beginning of their history. . . . Therefore
John, in the Gospel which bears his name, relates the
things done by Christ, when the Baptist had not yet
been thrown into prison ; but the other three evangelists
call to mind the things that were done after the imprisonment of the Baptist.   One who has given his attention to
these considerations can no longer suppose that the
Gospels are at variance with each other, since the Gospel
according to John includes the first of Christ's acts, and
the others the history that took place at the end of the
time.   It was natural then that John should pass over in

silence the genealogy of our Saviour, since it has been
written by Matthew and by Luke, and should begin with
the doctrine of the Divine Nature, since that had been
reserved for him, as for a superior, by the Divine Spirit.

(Eusebius, *Hist. Eccles.*, iii. 24.)

INDEX

Acts, accuracy of author, 17 ff, 250
  „ , aim of author, 247–248
  „ , discrepancies with epistles, 20, 21, 230–233
  „ , historical value of, 248–252
  „ , sources of, 241–244
  „ , speeches in, 231–232
  „ , v. also Luke-Acts
Advent, 22–23, 25–27, 119
  „ v. Parousia
Alexandrian text, 7 ff., 208
  „ thought, in Hebrews, 131, 140
  „ thought, in John, 270
Anti-Christ, in Apocalypse, 292–293
  „ , in Matthew, 223
  „ , in 2 Thessalonians, 27
Anti-Marcionite Prologue, to John, 274 n.
Anti-Marcionite Prologue, to Luke, 223 n., 239 n.
Anti-Marcionite Prologue, to Mark, 206 n.
Antioch, 199, 221–222, 239 n.
Antiquities, v. Josephus
Apocalypse, v. Revelation
Apocalyptic, in Mark, 206, 207, 210
  „ , in Matthew, 223, 224
  „ , in 1 Peter, 163
  „ , in 1 Thessalonians, 20, 22, 23
  „ , in 2 Thessalonians, 25–27
Apollos, and Corinth, 29, 30, 33, 34
  „ , and Hebrews, 131, 136, 137
Aquila and Priscilla,
  at Corinth, 28, 29
  at Ephesus, 72
  at Hebrews, 137–139
  at Rome, 59, 62

Aramaic in Mark, 184, 209
  „ original of Matthew, 216 ff.
  „ origin, of Gospels, 267
  „ „ , of John, 267
Aristion, and ending of Mark, 214
  „ , and 1 Peter, 158
Athanasius, Canon of, 13
Augustine, and Canon, 171, 293, on 2 John, 281

Bacon, B. W., on Mark, 208, 210
  „ , on Matthew, 222 n.
Baptist, and Fourth Gospel, 271
Barnabas, Epistle of, 12, 88, 135, 145
  „ , and Hebrews, 135
Baur, F. C., on Galatians, 54
  „ , on Romans, 66
  „ , on Thessalonians, 19
Bell, H. I., and Skeat, T. C., *Fragments of an Unknown Gospel*, 268, 273
Beloved Disciple, 255, 261
Bengel, on Corinthians, 33
  „ , on Philippians, 107
Bernard, J. H., *Commentary on St. John*, 257, 291
  „ , on authorship of Fourth Gospel, 259
  „ , on martyrdom of John, 257
  „ , on misplacements in Fourth Gospel, 268
Blass, F., on sources of Acts, 243
  „ , on Western text of Acts, 244–245
Bultmann, R., *Formgeschichte*, 201 ff.
  „ , Gallio, 28 n.
Burkitt, F. C., *Christian Beginnings*, 53, 64, 149

317